METAPHYSICS AND THE COSMIC ORDER

JOSEPH MILNE

Metaphysics and the Cosmic Order

☙❧

WITH A FOREWORD BY
HRH THE PRINCE OF WALES

AND AN INTRODUCTION BY
JOHN O'DONOHUE

TEMENOS ACADEMY

TEMENOS ACADEMY PAPERS NO. 27

This paper comprises four lectures,
revised into book form,
delivered to the Temenos Academy
at the Essex Unitarian Church, London
during the Lent Term 2006

First published 2008 by
The Temenos Academy
16 Lincoln's Inn Fields
London WC2A 3ED

www.temenosacademy.org

Registered Charity No. 1043015

The Temenos Academy wishes to thank an anonymous donor
for generously sponsoring the publication of this book.

Cover image
Eriugena's fourfold division of nature (God, the primary causes, effects,
and unformed matter) as depicted by Honorius Augustodunenis
in his *Clavis physicae*, Paris Bibliothèque Nationale, Latin 6734, 3 verso
(Photograph by permission of the Bibliothèque Nationale)

Typeset by
Agnesi Text, Hadleigh

Printed in the United Kingdom at
Smith Settle, Yeadon

Dedicated to

KATHLEEN RAINE

bearer of light in an age of forgetting

Contents

 හ

Foreword

HIS ROYAL HIGHNESS THE PRINCE OF WALES

ᏄᏍ

I AM delighted to have this opportunity to provide a Foreword for this collection of essays which were originally given by Dr Joseph Milne as lectures at The Temenos Academy. For, by putting into a historical yet timeless context something that I have, as it were, always understood intuitively, Joseph Milne has made clear to us what we had, perhaps, forgotten. And that is that the language of scientific empiricism which so dominates our contemporary discussion is not the only language that we might choose to guide us, but is one that is best used—and, indeed, should only be used—in rather particular circumstances. That is to say that whilst it is undoubtedly necessary, it is not in any way sufficient.

Joseph Milne proposes three possible kinds of knowledge that can be differentiated from each other. These are: the religious, the philosophical and the empirical. Each of these has a particular manner and scope—religious knowledge reveals the sacred presence in all things; philosophical knowledge is concerned with meaning and provides us with the metaphysical understanding of the essence of reality; and empirical knowledge, which comes from the realm of observational deduction of the laws and nature of visible reality, is the knowledge of the empirical sciences. Each of these kinds of knowledge opens up different aspects of reality and can easily mislead if used to tackle questions that lie beyond their proper scope.

If we more readily recognize the last of these orders of knowledge—that of scientific empiricism—it is because our contemporary Western society is largely dominated by it. However, this was not always so—and may not always be so in the future. Schooled as we are in the virtues of the Enlightenment, with its emphasis upon rational deduction and the understanding of the 'mechanics' of Nature—a focus upon the separate parts rather than the whole; an explanation of all that is in material terms—it is difficult for us to remember that there existed before that time (and remains, if we would but seek it) another coherent and well-formed body of thought and expression that, by contrast, is characterized by its emphasis upon integration, participation and wholeness.

Whilst the forms of enquiry that have developed from the Enlightenment have enabled us to achieve a great deal in terms of improving the material human condition, the shift away from our sense of participation in Nature to a claim of mastery and exploitation has reaped a bitter harvest. Indeed, as Joseph Milne suggests, this sense of mastery, when matched by an emphasis upon the Divine Will instead of the Divine Being as in earlier times, has proved critical. As he says in his first essay, the fundamental break between things known and the mind that knows has moved from the direct contemplation of reality, as an end in itself, to regarding Nature as a mere resource for human mastery and command:

> At a single stroke human nature is alienated from the cosmos. With this alienation, the conception of human knowing shifts from participation in the being of things to the mastery of the will over things.

As it happens, this matter of 'participation' and engagement has been something that I have felt deeply ever since I was a teenager, and I have tried to follow it in all the various practical ventures I have undertaken. In different ways, I have tried to do what I can to heal the wounds—to reconnect and to reintegrate that which has become so fragmented and deconstructed. Whether it be in terms of working with young people to offer them a start in life; or working with local people to enable them to have the kind of places in which they would like to live; or supporting the use of the best of traditional health care alongside conventional medicine; or, indeed, working with companies to encourage them to participate in their local communities, the root principles have been integration and harmony—following, if you like, Joseph Milne's proposition that 'all things are in communion with all other things' and that we are all 'called to bear witness to the truth of things'.

At the heart of all of this has been my underlying belief in a natural order and harmony that is both external and internal, a truth that is, of course, ever taught by the mystics and sages of all the great spiritual traditions. Alongside the brilliance of scientific enquiry, therefore, lies a timeless wisdom of the way things really are within, above and beyond all that we can know from our five senses.

I suppose that one of the most evident examples of our loss of harmony is shown in the crisis of environmental degradation and climate change. Part of the solution to this crisis will no doubt be technological, but part will need to be found in the realm of human values; the need for a reappraisal and rebalancing of our relationship with the natural order of Nature. Thus it is that the solution requires not only scientific enquiry but also matters that dwell within the scope of philosophy and religion. Somehow or other, and with mounting urgency, we have to rediscover that which we once knew— that, in reality, there is a relationship and correspondence between Nature and human society, and that the fragmentation and speciali- zation that is a characteristic of scientific empiricism needs to be balanced by that which fosters what is integrative and whole.

As Joseph Milne shows, there is no necessary conflict between the three kinds of knowledge. It is only when they become exclusive or fragmented that an apparent conflict appears. If science and techno- logy are pursued with reverence for Nature, as Einstein did for example, then the extraordinary order of Nature is revealed. But if the sciences are applied to Nature without regard for the whole, then some loss comes with each gain. There is no reason for the sciences not to work *with* Nature if the whole is kept in view.

But this also means that we have to keep human nature in view. The Scriptures say 'man does not live by bread alone', and, therefore, we might say in our age that man does not live by technology alone, but according to the inner truth of his being so that he feels himself part of the mysterious order of things. This means that we need to see human society as part of Nature, and not as some artificial imposition upon it. Plato, as Joseph Milne points out, saw society as a reflection of the cosmic order, and that good human laws corresponded with natural law.

Yet beyond even this there is the spiritual dimension to Man and Nature. The mystics and the greatest artists see Nature as the face of the infinite, as divine presence, in which all things are bound together in union and where the essential law is divine grace. From this point of view there is no conflict between the different kinds of knowledge, save in the manner they are pursued and the ends they seek.

Our fragmented view of the modern world is reflected in the fragmentation of the branches of knowledge, and the separation of knowledge from the meaning of our lives. In his final essay Dr Milne presents us with the challenge to understand not only the three different orders of knowledge, but to bring them into fruitful relation. He sees this as the call of our age.

These essays have struck a chord with me and confirm, in a scholarly way, what I have intuitively felt for many years and tried to apply in practical ways.

Introduction
Thinking: An Invitation to Presence

John O'Donohue

ফেC.

We often seem to undertake the longest journey in order to arrive at what has been nearest all along. This is the beauty of philosophy. In philosophy thought incarnates, unfolds and enlightens. When we enter into this we are awakened to the luminosity and mysterious intimacy of thought itself. In following thought towards the crests of infinity, we suddenly awaken, home in that recognition that our very being and presence unfolds and articulates itself in and through thought. There is no nearness nearer than thought; it is the mirror at the heart of presence. It might be often blurred but it is always implicitly there. When it brings us on an active and explicit voyage of thinking, philosophy manifests the holiness of thought. Ultimately, thought is the source unfolding itself.

If the activity of thought is that intimate and ultimate, then the deeper patterns of our complexity, behaviour and belief are to be sought in the concealed rhythms and habits of our thinking. This is exactly the claim of Joseph Milne's book. But it is not merely a claim; rather the content and form of this book are one. This is a book about thought wherein thought itself as text does exactly what the book claims. Though it is a short book, its range and depth are huge. It is written with a beautiful simplicity. Its tone is mild and the cumulative body of insight unfolds with great gentleness. A voice that is sure has no need to shout. Yet, as you read, you gradually realize that this is a subversive work that calls into question some of the key orthodoxies of contemporary thought, exposing the suppressed naivety of their assumptions and the confusion and category mistakes at the centre of their truth claims. The voyage of thinking undertaken so gently in this book reminds one of the old dictum about the capacity of art to conceal art!

Dr Milne shows a thorough acquaintance with the Western philo-sophical tradition. His grounding axiom is that the human sense of totality is in fact a pre-intuition of all that is. Human nature is intrin-sically bound up with the cosmos. He carefully distinguishes the primary ways our knowing configures itself: the religious, the philo-sophical and the empirical. Each way of knowing is also a different style of orientation towards, and engagement with, reality. Each of these approaches delivers a different kind of truth. Dr Milne outlines clearly and rigorously the different styles and rhythms of knowing that each involves. In this way, he creates clear and generous thought-space for the uniqueness of each approach to be honoured; yet he is always careful to underline the capacity and limitation inherent in each approach. Having achieved such an honourable sense of the contour of each way of knowing, his lucid and imaginative analysis liberates each approach to engage with each other in the deepest potential of conversation and question.

In a time that lives under the unquestioned despotism of the *how*, it is so refreshing and liberating to undertake the thought-voyage on which he invites us. This enables him to make a wonderful clearance in the dogmatism of modern empirical science which arrogantly engages in a claim-making way that is too frequently beyond its capa-city and remit. Into what often feels like a matrix smothered in dog-matic cellophane, he brings the oxygen of true speculative thought.

Identifying the fatal flaw/fall in the tradition, namely, the shift from ontology to the lonely imperialism of volition, he restores autonomy and freedom to the act of knowing, revealing its ground and calling within the larger subjectivity of being itself. He shows how 'know-ledge belongs to the intelligence within things. The act of being is simultaneously an act of self-disclosure.' He supplements this insight with the coy but penetrating recognition that space itself is a mode of being. While his insights here are philosophical reflection of a high order claiming, for instance, that 'the human act of knowing has meaning for the things known', it is also a deeply poetic insight that reaches to the heart of the poetic calling and process. In the *Duino Elegies*, Rilke said:

Could it not be that we
are here to say: house,
bridge, cistern, gate,
pitcher, flowering tree,
window—or at most:
monolith . . . skyscraper?
But to say them in a way
they, themselves, never
knew themselves to be?

(Rilke: *Ninth Duino Elegy*
translated by Robert Hunter)

His book is no innocent throwback to pre-modernity; it does not naively want to restore classical metaphysics. This is thinking that is wide awake to the tortuous thought-journey of modernity and post-modernity; consequently, it is thinking that is wide awake to itself. It is in the tradition of the Platonic Dialogues, rigorous and imaginative speculative conversation that offers a new ground of unity to integrate our fragmented discourse and enable us to forge a new beginning. It is a true invitation to the adventure of thought. Its implications are also profoundly ethical in that it invites the fullest realization of individuation but in creative tension with the full and unfolding substance of the communal.

At a time when no frontier seems sacred, this careful and penetrating book offers us new lenses through which we may see things anew, adjust our misguided hubris and develop a style of thinking that will open to us the full adventure of knowing. It accords to the act of knowing a profound emergent creativity that serves the actualization and realization that sleeps so lightly within the call of creation. As he says: 'every word we speak is our *reply* to existence.' To put it differently, this book is a wonderful portraiture of the wholesomeness that resides so deftly and obliquely at the heart of all thought, feeling, discourse and action. The true act of thought discloses this creative embrace and is itself, in fact, called forth by it. This book is like a prism working inwards, it can illuminate our contemporary thought-fractures in their full edge and colour because it portrays them against their originary home-light.

Read this book once through quickly; then, return and travel slowly with a careful and subtle mind. Allow your own thought to be quickened, challenged and transformed. In these fractured times, Dr Jospeh Milne offers us a book that is a live event of challenging and redemptive thought.

1

Human Understanding and the Cosmos

ଚଡ଼

O NE of the distinguishing features of human nature is that it seeks to understand the nature of the cosmos, the order of the universe in its totality. This quest for understanding shows itself in every civilization and culture from the most ancient to the present day. Indeed, we may say that the manner in which a civilization conceives the cosmos fundamentally informs every other aspect of its life and culture. Any major changes in culture are grounded in changes in the way the cosmos is conceived. This is the case in our own age just as in any previous time.

In these four lectures we shall ask what it means that mankind considers the cosmos. I feel this is a very important question in our time. We live in an age dominated by science and technology and these are now largely shaping how we consider the cosmos. With this dominance of the material sciences the various other ways the cosmos has been conceived down the ages are being pushed aside and classified as either primitive science or superstitious myths. But even within the natural sciences there are conflicts about the interpretation of the universe and of evolution, as well as conflicts between physics and biology. But also, at this time, the West is absorbing cosmologies from the Eastern religions that are integral to their paths towards enlightenment. Consequently our thinking about the universe and the nature of reality is pulled in many different directions.

I must admit that I find the present confusion between different competing cosmologies fascinating. It seems to me worth asking why it is that our conceptions about the cosmos raise our passions, or cause us fear. Why does so much seem at stake in how we conceive the universe? I would suggest that, intuitively, we all sense that the shape, order and destiny of human society is bound up with it. I believe everybody feels this, even if they cannot articulate it in any detail. At an absolutely fundamental level human nature senses itself as bound up with the whole cosmos, despite the fact that this seems to have little to do with our everyday lives and activities. Yet it does. Our institutions, our laws, traditions, education and religions are all bound up with how the cosmos is conceived. And how mankind conceives itself is bound up with how the cosmos is conceived. Always, throughout history, there has been a relationship between the way in which the cosmos is conceived and the way in which human nature is conceived, and this is so in our time too. There is a correspondence between the depth of our vision of the universe and the depth of our own self-understanding. The 'sense of totality' and the 'sense of self' are two aspects of a single apprehension. The forms these take at any time determine the quality and nature of culture, its institutions and aspirations.

In our time, however, not only are there competing cosmologies, but also confusions between different modes of thinking about the cosmos. To help bring some clarity amid this confusion I propose to differentiate these different modes of thinking into three distinct categories or levels: Religious, Philosophical and Empirical. These three categories are broad, yet quite distinct from one another. They are three discrete levels of apprehension and they stand in hierarchical order, one above the other, not alongside each other. I suggest the Religious, Philosophical and Empirical because we can see at a glance that much confusion arises through mixing them up, or from judging one in terms of another. That is evident in the current debate between the theories of Intelligent Design and Darwinian evolution, where the symbolic sense of the Scriptures is being confused with science. Rather less apparent, however, is the philosophical confusion of science and metaphysics, though it can be seen in the fascination with quantum physics and its erroneous alignment with metaphysics. We shall return to that problem later. For the present I wish to keep these three levels quite distinct from one another because they are wholly different ways of apprehending, thinking and knowing.

It will be helpful to clarify the three levels. By the Religious I mean the revelatory, sacred Presence in all things, the disclosure of the created realm as an act within the mind of God. I include here every form of theophany or hierophany to the total absorption of the soul in transcendent mystical union, and every form of emanation and transcendence. From this level come all the various 'sacred cosmologies' that are symbolic articulations of the divine ground of all that exists.

By the Philosophical I mean the metaphysical understanding or contemplation of the essence of reality. We include here epistemology—the science of knowledge—ontology—the science of being, and teleology—the science of ends.

By the Empirical I mean the entire realm of observational and inferential deduction of the laws and nature of visible reality, the realm of the empirical sciences, of 'objective' knowledge. From this we formulate the theories of how things are.

These three levels are not merely three types of representation. They are distinct modes of orientation towards reality, or kinds of engagement with the cosmos. The Genesis story of creation, for example, cannot be put alongside modern evolutionary theory because they spring from entirely different orientations towards reality. Scientific evolutionary theory springs from inference from precise observation of the structure and processes of nature or the material realm. The Genesis story, on the other hand, belongs to the founding myth of a people articulating the existential relation of humanity as such to the call of the Infinite beyond the created order. Religion always has at its heart the relation of the created and the uncreated, or the relation between that which 'is' and that *prior* to all that is. This is not a theoretical position. It emerges directly from the nature of human consciousness as such, which has a pre-intuition of the ineffable that lies ontologically prior to existence, yet which calls existence to itself, and is that for which all things have come into being.[1] Human

---

1. By 'pre-intuition' I refer to a fundamental insight of Western philosophy which is to be found expressed, in one way or another, from the Presocratics until the

consciousness knows it stands immediately before the eternal and ineffable, as well as before the world. The religious creation myths and cosmogonies are concerned to articulate this ultimate mystery in which human consciousness stands. These myths are existential narratives and, as such, they are entirely symbolic. To read the Genesis creation story as literal history is to read it non-religiously and quite naively. The same is true for all other creation myths that belong to the founding narratives of the different religions. Each is symbolic and we cannot reconcile one symbol with another because each speaks into a different human situation, and because they are narratives of concern, not of facts. They intimate something beyond themselves. In this sense they stand at the opposite pole to the sciences, which aim to represent the visible world directly and without ambiguity.

Philosophy stands intermediate between the Religious apprehension and the Empirical apprehension of things. Strictly speaking, it is concerned with metaphysics, which means the entire realm of conscious being, or ontology, or being reflecting on itself. Although modern philosophy extends itself into many different fields of enquiry, nevertheless it remains rooted in the reflection of being upon itself and ceases to be philosophy if it strays into empiricism or religion. There is a qualification to this, however. Since philosophy reflects upon being knowing itself, it necessarily reflects upon the meaning of knowing. Therefore it is philosophy that reflects upon the manner of knowing that belongs, for example, to the empirical sciences. The sciences take as given the methods applied in its investigations of things. Science cannot investigate the *meaning* of science or the nature of knowing. Nor can the sciences investigate the relevance of science to mankind. The sciences do not and cannot reveal the *meaning* of things. That enquiry belongs to philosophy. Just as when

---

Renaissance, in which it is understood that 'thought' originates in reality itself and is integral to reality itself. It means that 'mind' and 'knowing' are primordially the same, and that it is this knowledge which philosophy was always concerned to bring into active reflection and articulation.

religious creation myths are taken to be literally true they are falsified, so likewise scientific facts are no longer properly scientific when taken to reveal the meaning of things. The realm of meaning belongs to philosophical reflection and ultimately to the realm of being reflecting on itself. This becomes obvious to us when ethical questions about the use of scientific knowledge confront us—for example human cloning, or eugenics in medicine. Ethical questions are *human* questions, not scientific ones. They are existential, not empirical.[2] They cannot be answered through any logical or calculative method.

Because philosophy is grounded in the reflection of being upon itself, it therefore belongs to all humanity. This is important. The highest religious knowledge of God comes by the grace of the Infinite itself, and in this sense is not at the command of the human person. On the other hand, scientific knowledge is, theoretically, open to all who master its methods, but not to those who do not. It belongs to specialists. Philosophy, however, is neither given as a gift of grace, nor through the mastery of method. It is open to all and belongs to nobody in particular. This is because we are all beings who belong to the realm of being, and are therefore already reflecting on being. Our everyday lives are the direct encounter with being, and we naturally reflect on this. Our reflections may not be equal to that of the great philosophers or, more probably, we may not have their capacity to fully articulate our insight into things. Nevertheless, we can engage in the works of the great philosophers and recognize their insights, just as we can recognize the insights of the great poets. In this sense the philosophers speak for us, in so far as we recognize the truth or falsehood in what they say.

Here we must make a further distinction. Philosophy is not the formulation of theories about things. It may *consider* theories about things, but its task is not to formulate them. Its task is to bring to light that which being shows out of itself, so that it may be recognized. Its work is always to go beyond theories to things themselves.

---

2. For a detailed study of the problems of modern ethical thinking see Alasdair MacIntyre, *After Virtue* (Duckworth, 1985).

When philosophy fails to do this it falls away from metaphysics. This falling away from metaphysics is a particular problem of philosophy in our time and we shall return to it in the final lecture.

I have already said a few things about science. We observed that science cannot discern its own nature. This has been noted by modern philosophers[3] and there is a considerable literature of the philosophy of science which tries to bring to light the nature of science and the nature of human investigation of nature through science. There are two principal areas of general confusion about the natural sciences. The first is the assumption that they can disclose the metaphysical dimension of things, or can answer metaphysical or theological questions. It is here that we encounter the conflict between religion and science.[4] We noted that the religious creation myths should not be understood as literal, historical facts. They are symbols. Symbolic understanding should not be confused with scientific understanding. The present disputes over the biblical story of creation and the scientific theories of evolution demonstrate a confusion on both sides.[5] Both parties are reading the myth as literal history. The fault here, strictly speaking, lies with the religious side of the debate for not making it clear that the biblical account of creation is an existential symbolic narrative of the human relation with the Infinite. As strict fact it has no meaning. But this confusion lies in yet another misreading of things. The 'origins' of the universe that science seeks to uncover are not origins in the biblical or religious sense. For science the origins of things means the discernment of the temporal unfoldment of nature, the sequence in chronological time through which the forms of nature emerge, and the processes or

3. See especially Heidegger, *The Question Concerning Technology and Other Essays* (Harper, 1977).

4. Scientists rarely debate with philosophers. A good example of such a dialogue and its difficulties is *What makes us Think?* by Paul Ricoeur and Jean-Pierre Changuex (Princeton, 2000).

5. I refer to the debate between the Christian fundamentalist literal reading of *Genesis* that opposes any evolutionary theory and Richard Dawkins who likewise reads *Genesis* literally, for example.

mechanisms by which they emerge. Origins in the biblical or religious sense, on the other hand, means the immediate ontological presence of the cosmos in which human consciousness finds itself called to make response. This has nothing to do with the chronological time of science. On the contrary, it stands vertically directly in line with eternity. Origin in this sense is always present. It is concerned with the sacred meaning of things, and is therefore necessarily symbolic. Science and religion are dealing with two quite distinct kinds of truth, and there is no necessary conflict between them. There cannot be a conflict between different orders of truth. This was always understood by the ancient philosophers, such as Plato and Aristotle, or by theologians of the Middle Ages such as Aquinas. The confusion of different orders of knowledge or understanding is a specific problem of our age and calls for the very serious attention of scholars.

This problem has arisen because of a second difficulty which is harder to unravel. Science is a method of empirical investigation. Taken simply as that it presents no difficulty whatsoever. However, *in practice* modern scientific enquiry is invested with an ideology which is not part of science at all. It is believed that the empirical investigation of nature will prize open its secrets and place them at human disposal. This idea was expressed right at the birth of modern science in the writings of Francis Bacon, who declared that the object of knowledge is the control of nature which, of itself, has no purpose.[6] It is this intention through which scientific investigation is undertaken that presents the really serious problem of modern science. The notion that nature has no purpose in itself, but may be rendered useful to man, is a major change in thinking of the cosmos. It is this new orientation towards nature that marks the birth of the modern age, not the rise of the sciences as such.

It is quite clear, however, that the religious cosmologies are not in any sense connected with the idea of gaining mastery over nature. On

6. For a discussion of the move from contemplative knowledge to utilitarian knowledge see Louis Dupré *Passage to Modernity* (Yale, 1993), Chapter 3, 'The Emergence of Objectivity' in which Bacon's scientific ideology is discussed.

the contrary, they are concerned with the religious question of how man may conform his being and actions to the sacred order of things and sanctify them. Looked at this way the cosmos discloses itself entirely differently to the way it discloses itself through the natural sciences. Nevertheless, the ideology of mastery over nature need not rule the sciences, and empirical enquiry into nature could be undertaken for different reasons, and that could disclose nature differently. Such a change, however, could come about only through a transformation of the way our modern culture conceives how human existence relates to the cosmos or participates in the larger design of reality. What is clear is that the *manner* in which the sciences are undertaken determines where they look and what they can see. It is not the method as such that determines this. It is the idea or claim that scientific method somehow 'does itself' which conceals the way in which the community elects where it is applied. This process of election is very complex because it embodies the spirit of the age, and the spirit of the age is the gathering of all the concerns which are considered worthy of human effort and dedication.

In outlining these three modes of knowledge I have noted various problems that come with them, in particular that of confusing them together. In so doing I do not mean to critique them. In the very nature of things, human enquiry stumbles and feels its way only tentatively. It would seem, as the philosophers said long ago, that the knowledge of things is inexhaustible, even within the finite realm. And yet, as previously observed, there is the human sense of totality, a pre-intuition of all that is, of everything. This sense of 'the All' appears to belong to the nature of human consciousness as such, which is open to unlimited horizons, even to the wholly incomprehensible and to absolute nothingness. It stands, so to speak, at the centre of an infinite circle of potential knowledge. Therefore whatever is known in particular detail is also known to stand within the infinite horizon of all that is.

Given this there arises the peculiar question of where the human quest for knowledge might ultimately arrive. Is there necessarily always to be a disproportion between the presently known and the infinite ocean of possible knowledge? If that were so, then there would be no resting place for intelligence or consciousness. It is sometimes said, 'We can't know everything', but that reply betrays itself in using the word 'everything', since without the sense of totality that word could not be uttered. But there is something very important hidden in that reply: the notion that the pursuit of knowledge or truth is solely a matter of human will.

We need to consider that notion carefully. It is true that the desire to know belongs to human nature, and that that desire extends infinitely. Its object is the knowledge of everything. There is no reason to suppose, however, that the desire to know belongs simply to human subjectivity without a real relation to the existence of all things. The subjective conception of the ground of desire is a modern idea which springs from the Enlightenment dualism between mind and cosmos. The notion of closed human subjectivity runs through all modern thinking in one way or another, as if it were a self-evident truth. It is perhaps the single notion that marks the break with the Middle Ages all the way back to early Greek philosophy. It assumes a fundamental break between things known and the mind that knows, formulated in the Kantian notion that things cannot be known in themselves. At a single stroke human nature is alienated from the cosmos. With this alienation, the conception of human knowing shifts from participation in the being of things to the mastery of the will over things. Thus, as observed earlier, the quest for knowledge moves from the contemplation of reality, as an end in itself, to subjecting the resources of nature to human mastery and command. Knowledge is no longer for *the sake of things themselves*, but for human benefit alone, and therefore divorcing the human good from the universal good. The will to power, utilitarianism, pluralism, relativism and so on are all bound up with the alienated, self-enclosed human subject, in which the self itself is empty of any actual content and so must invent itself. Disconnected from any universal purpose in the fabric of things, the modern self is necessarily a vacant self.

This emergence of the will to know (displacing the call to know) has its origins prior to Descartes and Kant, however. In the late

Middle Ages the theologians began to conceive of God in terms of Divine Will instead of Divine Being. We see Bonaventure, Scottus and Ockhem all grappling with the problem of predestination and the relation of the 'reason' in things to the 'divine reasons' of things in the mind of God. Augustine had already situated 'the Fall' in the deviant human will and thus created a rift between human will and the Divine Will, thereby shifting the relationship between the human and the divine from that of ontology to volition. Thus will becomes implicitly separate from being and from knowledge, and being and knowledge become subservient to will. Bonaventure restores will to being through his understanding of Divine Love as the power that draws all things to unity in the Mind of God, and through his emanationism which sees the visible realms and the interior realm of the soul as 'traces' of the Divine Trinity.

Nevertheless, despite the restoration of the emanationist ontology at the close of the Middle Ages, the move from being to will was already seeded, and with the rise of the utilitarian ideology of knowledge, and the notion that nature was void of inherent purpose, coupled with the questioning of the absolute authority of the Church, the scene is set for the rift between human nature and the cosmos. With this move the relationship of human nature and the Creator shifts from that of participant in the mind of God to obedient subject outside God. The hierarchy of Being down to beings was broken. Man and cosmos stand outside the emanation of being and become merely the objects of divine intention.

I am abridging a complex transition of theological thought here, but the outcome is that man, as the image of God, becomes man the image of the will of God. In other words, the relationship of God to man becomes mirrored in the relationship of man to the cosmos. This conception of God prevails in modern religious thought, in which God is conceived merely as the external cause of things. Any conception of theocracy is framed in terms of will and obedience to will. God ceases to be the life of things and becomes the Lawmaker. It is this conception of God that lies at the heart of the debate over Intelligent Design and Darwinian evolution. But one can also see how the same conception lies at the heart of all modern moral thinking, the notions of human rights and freedom, the prevailing individualism, the abuse of the resources of the earth and so on. The key in each instance is the sovereignty of will.

It is therefore not surprising that the human quest for knowledge is presently conceived as springing solely from subjective desire. If the subject is essentially apart from all things and all it may look upon, this conception seems inevitable.

Nevertheless, it is a false conception. Not only does it run counter to the long theological and philosophical tradition of the West, it runs counter to reason itself. Clearly we cannot simply return to a previous age or merely take up ideas that cannot be located in the spirit of our age. We need to see things in a different way for ourselves. I believe there is a way out of our situation if only we could articulate that which we already know in our heart of hearts. Towards this end, I would like us to consider four propositions which we shall return to throughout these lectures. I am not going to present any new ideas, but rather draw upon ideas which have always been in our tradition in one way or another but which have been long overlooked.

> The first proposition is that mind or consciousness is already
>   connected with everything.
> The second proposition is that all things are in communion
>   with all other things.
> The third proposition is that all things disclose their nature
>   as an act of their being.
> The fourth proposition is that man is called to bear witness
>   to the truth of things.

These propositions are related to each other and are co-dependent. They are all to be found in the thought of Western[7] theology or philosophy, even if dispersed in different places and times.

---

7. In what follows, and throughout these lectures, I am confining discussion to Western culture because the problems I wish to address are part of the fabric of

The first proposition, that mind is already connected with every-thing, is to be found in different formulations in the Presocratic philosophers, Plato and the Neoplatonists as well as Medieval theo-logy. Intelligence or reason was always understood to be a universal until the Enlightenment.[8] The cosmos was understood to be intel-ligent, and human intelligence could discern the order of things because it too shared in the universal intelligence. The soul or psyche was the link between the body and mind, and hence the link between the particular and the universal. This means that 'knowledge' or 'gnosis' in the Greek sense belonged to the intelligence within all things, and that is why the highest form of knowledge was under-stood to be of universals, that is, the purely intelligible. And universals are known only through participation in their being.

It is because this understanding became gradually lost in Western thought that God became conceived as outside the cosmos, remotely directing it according to His will and no longer present in His being. Although the Christian and the Greek ways of expressing this under-standing are different, in essence they are speaking of the same in different aspects.

Western thought and their remedy needs to be found within that fabric. This is especially the case with regard to Western philosophy, which still remains in the ethos of ancient Greek philosophy.

8. The subject/object dualism, which we generally associate with Descartes and Kant, has its origins in the theological shift of conceiving God in terms of Will and no longer in terms of Being. Philosophy subsequently shifts from meditation on ontology to epistemology because the central problem now resides in the human 'will to know'. The object of knowledge, now framed in terms of that over which the mind can have command, is no longer an ontological entity, a being along with the being of man, but a set of abstracted properties known only in terms of subjective concepts or representations. Epistemology becomes mere representation. Thus there is no 'communion' with things through which they become known through their own disclosure of themselves. This epistemological emphasis has persisted until recent times, even though philosophers such as Schleirmacher or Kierkegaard, seeing its limitations, had struggled to overcome them. But their thinking also remained within the orbit of epistemology and never approached ontology outside the realm of human subjectivity. The return to ontology arrives with Husserl and Heidegger as a response to the problematics within philosophy itself.

The second proposition, that all things are in communion with all other things, follows from the knowledge or essence of things being universal. This is a property of being as such. If all beings did not share being in common, then everything would be closed in itself in an isolated existence of its own, without any relation to anything whatsoever. There would be no proportions or relations or processes or awareness between things. Modern thought tends to conceive the relations between things spatially, but the ancient understanding was ontological, where space too is a mode of being.

The third proposition follows on from this, that all things disclose their nature as an act of their being. This means that being is more than simple existence or passive thereness. It is an act within itself and out of itself, in which 'presence' as such is the act of being present *in* being and *before* and *towards* being. Or, to put it another way, the act of being is at the same moment the act of self-disclosure.

We shall return to these propositions in more detail later. For the present I wish only to relate them to the question of the desire or will to know. We observed that the modern notion of the desire to know is located in the subjective human will, in a world where there is no relation between the knowing subject and the things known. This makes all knowledge merely representations of things. But according to our third proposition, all things are disclosive of themselves as a property of their being as such. If that were not so there would be no objects to enquire into. Nothing whatever would be present before human intelligence, not even through mediation. But not only are all things disclosive of themselves, self-communicating, they are all in communion with one another.

The cosmos is in existence at once and at a single stroke. It is a unity. Bits of it do not come into existence independently but out of one another and according to one another. This interdependence of things has long been known in ancient forms of medicine, for example, and even in modern biology (despite what I said earlier about the sciences) the biological interdependence of things is beginning to emerge into view, not only among present living things in the biosphere, but through time and the sequences of development through time. Biological time is different from chronological time.[9]

So the question now arises as to what kind of knowledge presents itself, through the very nature of things, to human intelligence? And what, in this understanding of things, moves the desire for knowledge? It is a fairly basic rule that desire arises through attraction. It does not move itself, but is drawn forth by its object. This means that the knowledge in things is what attracts the human intelligence, rather than the will to gain mastery over things. Furthermore, the knowledge in things, which draws the mind to unite with them, is the *kind* of knowledge that already links the mind to things—that is to say, the knowledge which discloses itself.

Understood in this way there is a reciprocity between all things that are and the human mind. But more than this. Since the human intelligence is already a part of the totality of things, it has arisen in the cosmos in order that the self-disclosure of things is received.[10] This indicates that the human act of knowing has *meaning for the things known*. In some mysterious way the cosmos is served and gathered into itself through being known. It is part of the actualization of things.[11]

Such a reciprocity between 'knowing' and 'being known' is certainly foreign to the modern notions of epistemology. Nevertheless it brings us to our fourth proposition—that man is called to bear witness to the truth of things.

If we set aside the limited idea that the desire for knowledge is merely for the knower—a notion that follows from the supposition that consciousness is an *epiphenomenon* or unessential characteristic of the cosmos—it is possible to consider how knowing the truth of things has meaning within the totality of things. Indeed, why should that which encompasses everything have no part in everything? Without bearing witness to the truth of things there can be no

9. See Simon Conway Morris, *Life's Solution: Inevitable Humans in a Lonely Universe* (Cambridge, 2003).

10. See Josef Pieper, *Living the Truth* (Ignatius Press, 1989).

11. This is basic to the epistemology of Aquinas.

affirmation of being nor any creativity. Considered from this stand-point, every human endeavour *confers something* upon the cosmos. This is a property of every acknowledging, of every naming, and the very essence of the moral action.

The opening sentence of Aristotle's *Metaphysics* is 'All men natur-ally desire to know.' In his *Commentary* on this, Aquinas gives three reasons why this should be:

> The first is that each thing naturally desires its own perfection. Hence matter is also said to desire form as any imperfect thing desires its perfection. Therefore, since the intellect, by which man is what he is, considered in itself is all things potentially, and becomes them actually only through knowledge, because the intellect is none of the things that exist before it understands them . . . .
>
> The second reason is that each thing has a natural inclination to perform its proper operation . . . .. Now the proper operation of man is to understand, for by reason of this he differs from all other things . . . .
>
> The third reason is that it is desirable for each thing to be united to its source, since it is in this that the perfection of each thing con-sists. Now it is only by means of his intellect that man is united to the separate substances, which are the source of the human intel-lect and that which the human intellect is related as something imperfect to something perfect. It is for this reason, too, that the ultimate happiness of man consists in this union. Therefore man naturally desires to know.[12]

The first reason, that the intellect is potentially all things, and becomes them through knowledge and understanding, immediately grounds mind in everything that exists. Its potential to know arises from that which is to be known. This relates to what we called the pre-intuition of the totality of all things. The human intellect arises

---

12. Aquinas, *Commentary on Aristotle's Metaphysics*, translated by John P. Rowan (Dumb Ox Books, Notre Dame, Indiana, 1995) p. 3.

from that which is potentially to be known, which is the truth of things, and is actualized through understanding; and through understanding it participates in, or becomes, all things that exist. This, according to the second reason, is its proper operation, to which it is naturally inclined. But also, according to the third reason, the intellect desires union with its source, the substances of things, through which it is completed or actualized in itself. It becomes itself through union with what is. This also means that all things that exist are potentially united with the human intellect. Mind therefore confers knowing upon things, since in mind the things that exist receive reflection upon their existence. From this we can infer that mind has arisen from all existent things in order that they become known, and so that existence can bear witness of itself.

If we consider all the works of mankind from this perspective, then they may be seen as the embodiment of human understanding, or at any time the degree of understanding. This is especially so if we consider the arts and the institutions of civilization in their essential nature. They embody man's apprehension of the universe and his bearing towards all that is. The arts bear witness to beauty, politics and jurisprudence to justice, cultivation of the earth and medicine to the good, and learning to truth. The degree to which these each attain their ends depends upon the depth of intellectual receptivity to all that is which prevails at any time. Further, the community of mankind itself depends upon the common acknowledgement of the truth of things. Thus any disunity that may arise in human society will be due to a collective failure to acknowledge the truth of things, and this in turn will be reflected in a corresponding disunity with the cosmos or with the universal nature of things. Human nature and the cosmos are inextricably bound together.

2

Cosmos as Divine Revelation

&⊙&

I N the previous lecture we explored the question of the relation of
human understanding to the cosmos. We left a great number of
questions open. Here our theme is the cosmos as divine revelation,
which brings us to the essentially religious view of the cosmos.

Within Western civilization two currents of understanding have
run in parallel, occasionally coming together and parting again. The
first is what we might call the transcendent view of the cosmos, the
second what we might call the theophanic. In the first view the 'real'
is set wholly beyond the visible world of being and becoming, in the
One which is beyond all relations and all diversity. This view is most
elaborately set forth in Plotinus and later by Proclus. It is, we might
say, the most metaphysical view. The visible cosmos is, at best, a kind
of image of the One, or a sequence of realms that descend in order of
reality gradually from the One, terminating in nothingness, or which
ascend by degrees of reality terminating in the One.

The theophanic view, on the other hand, sees the cosmos as 'disclosure' of the divine, as the invisible made manifest. This view has
many variants or shades, ranging from the entire cosmos seen as divine
hierophany, as for example in Eriugena, to the breaking through of
the miraculous in holy showings, interventions or auguries. Essentially, this view grasps the visible as making present divine activity
and meaning, not merely as a 'standing for' the divine but the divine
actually manifest in some special sacred manner. To this manner of
seeing also belong the sacred arts and in particular what we may call
'poetic vision' which discloses through symbol rather than through
metaphysical or philosophical speculation.

As I said, the transcendent and the theophanic currents have always run parallel and occasionally converge. Yet their independence is obvious and they need to be kept distinct. One most important reason for keeping them distinct is that they arise from different modes of apprehension. What the poet or visionary sees is not what the philosopher sees, and they should never be explained in terms of one another. Poetry is not versifying metaphysical doctrines, and metaphysics is not rationalizing poetic vision. They each perceive the truth of things from different stances. Metaphysics proceeds by seeking the ultimate unifying principle concealed behind the visible or temporal, while the poet or prophet is granted by grace an immediate manifestation of the divine. Metaphysical understanding is won through deliberate discernment, while poetic vision is conferred as a gift from reality itself.

Another way of drawing this distinction is between the 'mythic' and the metaphysical. By the mythic I mean the special groups of stories that found a civilization or a religion and which are handed down through the ages in various forms and transformations and are generally gathered together as the founding literature of a civilization. In particular, I mean the various ancient cosmologies such as we find in Genesis or Greek mythology and the hymns to the divine powers or gods that accompany them. These myths embody symbolically the beginning of all things and the sacred order established throughout the created world which mortals are called to live by.

This mythic 'beginning of all things' is not, however, a chronological beginning, but rather the sacred pattern that underlies and governs the unfolding and meaning of temporal time. It crosses the motion of temporal time vertically and is present within it in all moments, uniting it in the eternal beginning or *arche* (ρχξ). A peculiar feature of these founding myths is that they embody in simple narratives the sum of all things at once. They are, so to speak, templates of the meaning of things, out of which may be drawn an almost infinite number of particular meanings. This characteristic also distinguishes them from metaphysical speculation. The mythic manner of apprehension grasps totalities instantaneously, while the metaphysical seeks to draw out the detailed order of relations from the One to the Many or of the Infinite to the finite. The 'abstract' language of metaphysics is quite foreign to the symbolic language of myth. In the mythic language the entire created realm reveals itself as saturated by divine meaning. The mountain, the sky, the ocean, the stars, stone, tree or bird are themselves the divine vocabulary of myth, disclosing meaning in their presence. This vocabulary belongs to what Kathleen Raine called 'the learning of the Imagination'. The world *speaks* a meaning which is at once temporal and eternal. Or as the philosopher Paul Ricoeur says:

> That a stone or a tree may manifest the sacred means that this pro-fane reality becomes something other than itself while still remain-ing itself. It is transformed into something supernatural—or, to avoid using a theological term, we may say that it is transformed into something superreal [*surréal*], in the sense of being super-efficacious while still remaining part of the common reality.[1]

The transformation of the profane reality into the supernatural is a mode of apprehension that occurs only through a special type of veneration for reality, in which precondition the sacred may disclose itself by an act of grace. Such seeing is always revelatory, a disclosure spontaneously *given* out of the reality of things, and is at once a transformation of the *seeing* as well as the seen. It is thus, as Ricoeur observes, the birth of ritual as well as myth. Through ritual remem-brance a people or a civilization maintains its association with the sacred manifestation through the profane reality of things. The ritual remembrance is a re-enactment of passing over from the profane to the sacred, and so holy places mark the threshold from profane to sacred. From this, Ricoeur and Eliade infer, all thresholds mark the passing over from one kind of space to another in which we take up a different relationship with our surroundings. This is so even down to the everyday threshold of the home. When we return to our homes each day we step over into a dwelling place with its own

---

1. Paul Ricoeur, *Figuring the Sacred* (Minneapolis, 1995), p. 49.

special sanctity, or likewise when we visit the homes of others we are guests by virtue of invitation into their special ground. This is also the case when we step into any institution. We enter into a relation with its own customs, manners and forms of conduct which situate us within a larger domain which can function only so long as the boundaries are respected or honoured. All customs and forms of conduct have their roots in the symbolic passing over from the profane to the sacred ground, and from this point of view any 'crime' is fundamentally a sacrilegious act, a disruption of the sacred order.

In our civilization there is a powerful myth which touches on this most profoundly and in all its magnitude. It is the story of the expulsion of Adam and Eve from the Garden of Eden. This myth may serve to illustrate what we observed a moment ago about symbols having almost infinite meanings.

The common literal interpretation of this myth takes it to be an historical event in which the Fall of Man brought evil and death into the world. Such a reading is far from the ancient way of reading it, and forgets it is symbolic. To take the myth as historical fact is to overlook entirely its embodiment of a symbolic meaning. Fact and meaning are not the same. The literal reading of this myth is perhaps the plainest example of the confusion of the different orders of knowledge, in this case the religious with the empirical.

Bearing in mind that meaning is always open and never fixed, closed or definitive, I would like to consider this myth for a few moments. First of all, we notice that there are two myths of the creation of Adam. In one he is created in the image of God, while in the other he is created from the dust of the earth, to which he shall return. Thus we have an 'immortal' Adam and a 'mortal' Adam, side by side. So the expulsion from the Garden cannot be taken literally to mean the fall into mortality. The two myths present Adam from two different angles. On the one side we have what has been called the state of Innocence, in which all things are given, while on the other we have Adam in the toil of labour and struggle. These two narratives present to us something central to the human situation, a state of completeness and a state of endless labour. We misread the myths if we suppose one follows after the other. Adam is presented to us as at once *finished* and yet *underway*.

The early Church has various ways of interpreting the Fall and the expulsion. One of the most interesting, which we find in the Greek Fathers and which recurs again in Swedenborg, is that Adam fell by attempting to understand divine matters through the senses rather than through the Intellect. This is interesting because the Intellect is understood as the power of the mind which apprehends the unity of things immediately and directly, while the senses can only infer from the multiplicity of things. Traditionally the Intellect is understood as the image of God in human nature. In the proper order of things, it is the Intellect that knows already the sacred nature of reality. This is what we referred to in the last lecture as the 'pre-intuition' of totality. The senses, and the intelligence that comes with them, on the other hand, tend to dispersion through the attraction of multiplicity— therefore the need to be ruled by the Intellect, or what has been called the 'inner Adam'.

Seen in this way the Fall is a forgetting of the given truth of things, which is the sacred knowledge, the knowledge that directly reveals itself to Adam, and which therefore requires no labour. This inter-pretation resonates with the Platonic view, that all real knowledge is recollection, while the knowledge derived through inference from the senses is at best only surmise or opinion.

We find this interpretation in Eriugena,[2] in the ninth century, who departed from Augustine's view that Adam once dwelled in Paradise as a historical fact. For Eriugena the Fall is Adam forgetting his own real nature, which is the image of God. He goes further and sees Paradise as the final destiny of humanity through the unfolding of eschatological time. Paradise is for Eriugena the knowledge of the ultimate end of man, the human vocation through sacred time. To forget Paradise is to forget the human vocation or calling, and there-fore to forget human nature itself.

2. Eriugena, *Periphyseon*, translated by John O'Meara (Bellarmin, Montreal, 1987), Book iv.

What is interesting in this way of seeing the Eden story is that 'gift' and 'labour' are juxtaposed. The sacred knowledge of things does not belong to the realm of labour, but to that of Grace. Adam is at once given all things, and yet also must labour. This corresponds to the cosmos itself, in the sense that the universe has come wholly into being as an act of creation, and yet it is also underway through temporal time in a process of becoming. So, from this perspective, what is Adam's labour? It would seem to be, in the most ultimate and holy sense, to return to God the gifts of his own hands. Or, in the language of the Scriptures, to make offering, and through that to sanctify the earth. In this way, the gift of receiving is made complete by the gift of returning, and the two aspects of Adam are united. The Fall therefore becomes the separation of the two aspects of Adam, which brings about simultaneously estrangement from God and estrangement from human nature.

This 'double estrangement', then, is the Fallen state. In this sense the Fall becomes the general human condition of estrangement writ large, so to speak. It is where humanity finds itself. It is where the two fundamental questions of spiritual union and the meaning of human work both emerge.

I stress that this interpretation is not definitive. It does not exclude other interpretations, or even render false interpretations that are inconsistent with one another. The kind of 'truth' that myths convey is not 'factual' in the empirical sense. They are symbolic narratives that bear meanings of an order which only narrative can convey, because a narrative bears and opens meaning in many directions simultaneously. Their meaning is ontological or existential rather than historical, in the sense that they bear meaning on the immediate human situation which is at the same time universal. The same may be said of all great stories or dramas.

This kind of interpretation, however, corresponds with the theophanic view of the cosmos, the view found in the early Fathers and revived by Eriugena in the ninth century. From the theophanic perspective nothing can be genuinely estranged from God because nothing exists outside of God. As Eriugena says:

... the Creative nature permits nothing outside itself because outside it nothing can be, yet everything which it has created and creates it contains within itself, but in such a way that it itself is other, because it is superessential, than what it creates within itself.[3]

All creatures exist within God, and because God wholly transcends all creatures He can at once be immanent in all creatures, and all creatures can be immanent within God. Eriugena draws from this a further quality of theophany:

> It follows that we ought not to understand God and the creature as two things distinct from one another, but as one and the same. For both the creature, by subsisting, is in God; and God, by manifesting himself, in a marvellous and ineffable manner creates himself in the creature . . . . [4]

Here the distinction between God's transcendence and immanence is identical with God as uncreated and as created. If nothing can exist outside of God, then neither can anything exist within God that is *other* than God. According to Eriugena God is wholly transcendent and wholly immanent, which is to say He is at once wholly unmanifest and wholly manifest. In such a view the Fall of Adam cannot be a corruption of nature, as Augustine thinks, which would mean the Fall of God in His manifestation, but rather that Adam forgets his nature and vocation and therefore the unity of his nature with God.

Given this forgetting and the consequent estrangement of Adam, the way is open for false unions. This opens up an aspect of the Old and New Testaments which is rarely touched upon—the symbolic meaning of false marriage or adultery. In forgetfulness, human nature seeks union blindly. We recall the story in the Gospel of John of the woman of Samaria who meets Jesus at the well of Jacob. Through a very strange discourse between the woman and Jesus, in which Jesus finally discloses himself as the Messiah, Jesus asks her to call her

3. *Periphyseon*, III.675C.   4. *Periphyseon*, III.678C.

husband. She says she has no husband, and Jesus says this is true, but that she has had five husbands. None of these are her 'true husband'. Early interpretations explain the five false husbands as the five senses, but now, before Christ, she comes to know both herself and Christ. She discovers she is the bride of Christ.[5]

A far more blatant myth of false union is found in the Genesis story of the building of the Tower of Babel. Here men are building a tower to reach up to heaven through their own inventions—with bricks instead of stones and slime instead of mortar. They are, as Sweden-borg interprets it, taking heaven by force.[6] That is to say, they are seeking heaven by their own devices while, in truth, it is given only by divine grace. Seen in this way, it is a most interesting parable about 'false labour', and how that leads to the confusion of tongues. This confusion of tongues, according to Swedenborg's interpretation, is the loss of the power to speak the truth, and that none could any longer understand another means the loss of the power to discern the truth of speech. It also means that speech in the mouth is split from the heart.

This division and confusion is yet a further instance of estrange-ment or alienation, both from God and within human nature. Again, I stress that this is just one way of reading these narratives. Neverthe-less, the theme of estrangement or alienation is one very clear way of discerning a consistency throughout the Scriptures, throwing a direct light on key symbolic themes such as adultery, idolatry, false witness and so on, all of which are acts of false relation with both God and the created order.

If the symbolism of the Fall suggests alienation as one possible sense, then the question of integration or participation arises. What does it mean for human nature to participate in the cosmic order? Earlier we touched on the threshold that passes over from the profane to the sacred. There is a parallel to this in the relation of human law

5. See, for example, the early Gnostic interpretation of this episode in Elaine Pagels, *The Johannine Gospel in Gnostic Exegesis* (Nashville and New York, 1973) p. 86.

6. Swedenborg, *Arcana Coelestia*, vol. 11 (London, 1978).

to cosmic law in Greek thought, which has been partly absorbed into Christian thought. This is the realm of what may be called natural law, which is bound up with the questions of providence and grace. Law, providence and grace are all ways in which the divine order is disclosed in nature.[7]

In Plato's Dialogues the question of the relation of human law and the law of nature recurs frequently in one way or another, commencing in an apparent contradiction between human law and nature. This contradiction presents itself in the notion that human laws are devised in order to protect the weak against the strong, while the law of nature favours only the strong. This idea lives on in modern thinking in the formulations of human rights and in social Darwinian theory. Nature and human society are regarded as essentially hostile towards one another for all but the strong or powerful, and therefore the formulation of human law is considered necessary to serve the function of protection from such hostility.

But for Plato and for Aristotle this view arises from a false conception of nature and the consequent false conception of human society. In nature all things serve the good of the whole. That, for Plato and Aristotle, is the fundamental law of nature. This means that the ends of all particular beings are bound up with the integration and harmony of the cosmos. There is a correlation between the natural fulfilment of the good of each being and the good of the whole. This is the fundamental ground of law in nature. All particular laws are ultimately subservient to this cosmic law of being as such.

Law, in this Greek sense, is essentially the *telos* or purposefulness of nature and all elements of nature. For each element or being to wholly actualize itself, to become fully itself, it must participate in the actualization of the whole cosmos. Aristotle formulated this principle in the following way: the essence of a thing is 'what it was for it to be'.[8] It means that the end or goal of anything is immanent in its essence,

---

7. See Fulvio Di Blasi, *God and Natural Law: A Rereading of Thomas Aquinas* (Indiana, 2006).

8. Quoted from Louis Dupré, *Passage to Modernity* (Yale, 1993), p. 26.

and that any process of development in nature is the actualization of the immanent end, its goal is the unfoldment of itself as fully what it is in relation to the entire unfoldment of all beings. Everything exists in its essence for the mutual good of everything. Consequently anything that exists simply for itself, regardless of the whole, can never actually come fully into being because it cannot participate in the *telos* of nature. This means that a human society that supposes each person may carve out a private destiny, regardless of the fulfilment of the whole, can only disintegrate. No being has a private destiny in its essence. It was for this reason that Plato dismissed democracy, in so far as democracy is conceived as the private will of individuals. The greater calling for society is to try to discern the correspondence between universal good and individual good. If this is not sought, then human society falls outside the greater design of nature and will, in effect, struggle against natural law. It will be ceaselessly trying to mitigate the ill effects of seeking ends foreign to the essence of human society itself.

It is important to appreciate that this is not an ideology. The correlation between the essence of each being wholly actualizing itself and the actualization of the whole cosmos depends upon conscious understanding. No social system can bring this about. At the same time, any social system will approximate the correlation to some degree or another and be, so to speak, an image of the cosmic order to some degree or another. Nevertheless, by the very nature of things, human society seeks this natural end. Every human being knows in their hearts that individual actualization is bound up with the totality of reality in some mysterious way, and that every natural human aspiration carries within itself the desire to participate in the whole of reality. This intuition encompasses at once the natural realm and the divine. In Greek thought we have to always keep in mind that there is no separation between nature and the divine, just as there is no separation between the human realm and nature as a whole. The cosmos is divine and the laws that work within it are not mere mechanical determinations but active divine intelligence. The cosmos is itself an intelligent being, manifesting that intelligence through all the orders of nature. Human intelligence naturally seeks participation in that universal intelligence.

In the first few centuries of Christian thought there was a great struggle to find adequate ways of conceiving the cosmos. Three different conceptions pull in opposite directions. First, the Biblical myth of creation does not envisage a cosmos in the Greek sense, complete and harmonious in itself. Second, the conception of the Fall implies that the order of nature is in some sense disrupted. Third, the Christ was conceived either as the Saviour who would re-fashion the world, or who would redeem humanity beyond this mortal world.

These three views present colossal problems for a religious tradition to sort out within itself, but since Christianity spread throughout the Greek and Roman worlds it had no choice but to confront all these difficulties, unless it was to become a religion merely for the uneducated. There were, however, elements already in the later books of the Old Testament which accommodated aspects of Greek cosmology, and also strains of Jewish thought that were absorbing Platonism, represented by figures such as Philo the Jew who gives a Platonic interpretation of Genesis.

I do not wish to trace out this complex history of thinking here. The central event of such thinking amounts to this: how may the mythological narratives inherited from Judaism be reconciled with the philosophical thinking inherited from Classical Greece? I observed at the beginning that the theophanic mode of representation was essentially symbolic, and this manner of thinking was quite different to the metaphysical manner of thinking. Symbolic understanding discerns a divine meaning manifest in visible things. Nature is a kind of theophanic vocabulary of the divine world. This is the mythic or poetic vision of things. The metaphysical view, on the other hand, takes the visible reality of things as directly disclosing their own essential nature. Here the world does not represent something beyond itself, but bears ultimate truth within itself through the contemplation of its own essence.

Clearly these two discourses can never be the same. They arise from different kinds of disclosure. Nevertheless they can become non-contradictory, and the long process of Christian thought until the close of the Middle Ages was, essentially, the enterprise of bringing about a synthesis of metaphysics and Scriptural revelation—what is called the relation of faith and reason.

At the risk of oversimplifying, I would like to draw to a close through the consideration of just one main element of this synthesis, but one to which scholars have not given due attention. It is the relation of actualization to redemption.

As we saw earlier, the Greek cosmos included all things. It is, essentially, the emanation of the One into the Many held together through form and proportion. The good of all things lay in each element actualizing its potential and thereby contributing to the good of the whole. This harmonious understanding of all natural development and fulfilment in the universal good showed that the laws of nature were also the laws of human society, and that there was no real division between divine law, natural law and human law. Christianity, on the other hand, saw the fulfilment of all through the divine intervention of Christ the Redeemer of Man from the Fall. In this, nature had no real part. The ills of human life were accounted for by the Fall and there had always been a tendency to discount 'this world' and place all hope in the next. Nevertheless, the doctrine of Redemption had its place in a larger eschatological history which saw eventually the renewal of all things in Christ and a return to the original condition of Paradise.

Thus the Greek understanding of the *telos* of all things towards their own perfection in the good, and the Christian understanding of restoration of all fallen things to their original good represent two different trajectories of time, one that draws all things to a future perfection, and one that returns all things to an original perfection. One trajectory of time is the goal of nature, the other the goal of grace. Both embody a conception of the fulfilment of all things, one through the actualization of essence through becoming, one through the restoration of nature through healing. Or again, potential and alienation stand as two orders of time through which perfection is to be attained.

Although there were moments of perceiving the convergence of these two conceptions of time, especially in the Greek Orthodox tradition, it was not until the eleventh and twelfth centuries that they were really conceived as convergent in the Latin tradition. Suddenly 'nature' was seen with new eyes. The Scriptures were the divine Word spoken in language, and nature the divine Word spoken in manifestation, as theophany. All things were in some sense a revelation of God.

It follows from this that everything created seeks two ends: its own full actualization as well as a return to its ground in God. A return to source and full actualization as created were two aspects of one divine journey. Or, in other words, the coming to fruition of the seeds of destiny and the 'gathering' of all things in time into mystical union with God, belonged together. Nature and grace are the two hands of time.

The coming into full actualization of being and the return of being to its ground in God are thus seen to be a single process. The two orders of time run concurrently. Everything *proceeds* from unity and *returns* to unity simultaneously, not sequentially. To divide these two processes into opposites deprives the cosmos of meaning. It renders creation as mere dispersion into multiplicity (a distorted kind of Platonism), and the return of all things into God as the mere negation of creation (a distorted kind of Christian theology).

Neither of these two kinds of time are time in the modern sense as mere interval between events. The modern conception of time, bereft of teleology or narrative, is not real time but a mechanistic abstraction of time. It is not even faithful to the observations of the sciences which discern organizing processes in the cosmos.

In closing, let me return to the four propositions we considered in the previous lecture.

Mind or consciousness is already connected with everything.
All things are in communion with all other things.
All things disclose their nature as an act of their being.
Man is called to bear witness to the truth of things.

From the first we have a metaphysical unifying principle from which the 'recollection' of the ground of all things arises. This accounts for the 'memory' of Paradise as the seed of time. From the second we have the 'intuition' of the mystical union of all things in the mind of God. From the third we have the metaphysical principle of the unity of being and becoming, or potential and actualization. From the fourth we have the metaphysical principle of the 'call' of human nature to understand and to make reply to the divine order of all things. This last principle is the one which unites all human creative endeavour with the return to the source of existence. It is the true essence of human labour.

Looked at in this way we see that these four principles completely reconcile becoming and return to source, creation and redemption. But also, in terms of our present theme, they reconcile nature and theophany. Symbolic apprehension and metaphysical apprehension are clearly distinct. One grasps a multiplicity of meanings at a stroke, while the other discerns the specific principles of things. Nevertheless they do not contradict one another, and at certain moments in our culture they converge. When that occurs we see the flowering of culture in all its richness and abundance, in the arts, learning and in mysticism.

3

Theology and Metaphysics

ଚଠ

IN our first lecture we distinguished three distinct modes of thought about the cosmos—the Religious, the Philosophical and the Empirical. We observed that confusion arises when these three modes of thought are mixed together. It is extremely important to appreciate that these are three different stances towards reality, concerned with different kinds of truth, different kinds of thinking or understanding. I would like now to draw out some of these differences more clearly. If we can properly distinguish them, then we may come to a position where we can see their relations to each other.

We observed two examples of confusion in our first lecture: the first was represented by the current dispute between the 'creationists' and the 'evolutionists', specifically in the debate about 'intelligent design'; the second was the claim that the 'new physics' revealed or corresponded with 'religious' or metaphysical truths about the universe.

The theory of Intelligent Design claims that, given the enormous complexity of the universe, of nature, of biology and so on, none of this order could exist without a supremely intelligent designer creating it. This position is essentially an empirical argument for the existence of God. It is not a new argument. It is what Aquinas calls the argument from causation,[1] namely that all effects have ordered causes and that causation must go back to some first cause of all things. However, conceived in this way the inference does not trace a way back to God, but only to a conception of efficient causality. Nothing is disclosed about the nature of God in the concept of causality. There

---

1. *Summa Theolgogia* 1a 2, 3.

is nothing in this argument to say that the cosmos, taken as a totality, is not self-caused. The evolutionists quite rightly say that 'causality' does not logically imply 'God' as the cause of things. Nor does the argument from complexity logically imply an intelligent designer outside the universe, since intelligence and complexity are integral to the cosmos itself and not imposed upon it.

But the real difficulty with such a way of thinking is that it conceives of God empirically, as merely the end-point in a series of empirically observed causes and effects. It does not move from the empirical realm to the religious in any way. Thus, as put forward by the proponents of Intelligent Design, it is no more secure as a theory of origins than any other scientific theory of origins. And by relegating 'intelligence' to a 'designer' outside the universe the theory places itself squarely within the secular Enlightenment world-view. There is no ontological connection between a designer God and the world. Religiously or theologically speaking, God is not an object of rational inference or logical demonstration. We shall see how this is so later.

The second claim, that the new physics reveals something religious about the nature of reality is a simple mistake of category, mixed with a fallacious conception of consciousness. First of all, physics does not move into the territory of metaphysics. That is the realm of being. No matter how subtle any theory of the order of things may be, it is never metaphysical. Secondly, the notion that in the new physics the method of enquiry 'influences' the phenomena observed has nothing to do with consciousness. It is the instruments that alter the phenomena, not the observer.

In saying this we do not mean to detract in any way from the scientific investigation of things. It is not the place of religion or theology to decide in any way the accuracy or otherwise of scientific investigation. But what religion or theology can say is that 'God' cannot be the object of empirical enquiry, no matter how such empirical enquiry is conducted. It is worth observing, in this regard, that the analytic school of philosophy, which models itself on the epistemology of empirical investigation, cannot demonstrate the existence of the universe, let alone the existence of God. There is no 'proof' of existence as such. This is because existence and being are *given in advance* of any enquiry. All empirical enquiry necessarily takes existence as such for granted, including the existence of the possibility of enquiry. There cannot be an argument for existence as such, if only because there has to be existence for there to be an argument. Here we find agreement with the logical positivists: that God is beyond demonstration. But I disagree with the positivists when they claim that logical demonstration is the only kind of knowledge. On the other hand, the proponents of Intelligent Design are inadvertently trying to place God in the realm of logical demonstration, in order to legitimize belief in God. The empirical argument for Intelligent Design is making the same logical error as the argument for atheism.[2]

The kind of difficulty we run into when the different orders of knowledge become confused is quite obvious in these examples. What is of interest here is that this problem has arisen through the prevailing popular belief that 'knowledge' is approached in only one way— namely through inference from evidence. It forgets that the empirical realm is but one aspect of reality, and in this forgetfulness it does not see that its method becomes falsified when applied outside the realm of the calculable.

But, as we have seen previously, there is an order of knowing which does not infer but which apprehends directly. This is the case with being or existence. But also the act of knowing apprehends itself directly. That is to say, knowledge of existence or being is already given to the mind, even in its own act. Being manifests itself. This is really the first principle of metaphysics. But also, being is known not only directly in its immediate presence to itself, it is also known already to be universal. That is to say, it is known that everything that is partakes of the act of being. Nevertheless, although being and the

---

2. Strictly speaking empirical methodology does not deal with either existence or being in the metaphysical sense of these terms. It takes as given the 'thereness' of things prior to the application of any method. There is no difficulty in this so long as it is remembered that it is not disclosing the thereness of things but discerning properties consequent upon thereness.

knowledge of being are given, the discernment of the meaning of being requires philosophical reflection. Such reflection is the specific task of metaphysics or ontology. This reflection cannot be undertaken using scientific method or through logical deduction from hypotheses. This is because nothing can be posited *prior* to being from which being may be deduced, and because the act of knowing and the act of reasoning are themselves bound up in the act of being. There is no objective standing outside being in order to observe it. The knowledge of being is from within being. A great deal of the confusion in modern thinking is simply due to failing to distinguish what is first given, which is the direct knowledge of universal being as such, without any distinction between subject and object. Subject and object can only be distinguished subsequently to the given knowledge of universal being as such. Neither the Cartesian self nor the logical positivist's objective reality are first in the order of knowledge.

Given this difference between empirical knowledge and metaphysical knowledge, we may ask what kind of knowledge arises from looking at the cosmos metaphysically. Traditionally, what shows itself in this way of seeing is that there are different modes of being and different orders of being. The manner of being of a plant is different to the manner of being of a dog. Because of this we comport ourselves differently towards a plant or a dog, and this act of human comportment towards beings is bound up essentially with the human mode of being. As Paul Tillich says, the human being is the being who asks the question of being,[3] which is possible only because the human being may reflect on being *as itself a manner of being*. For man, being is always underway in coming to know being. This, essentially, is how man participates in the world. Being is at once known and yet unfolding itself to human knowledge. This is the case both for the individual and for a civilization, and for this reason metaphysics can never be closed or finished. The various cosmologies of different civilizations or religions are grounded in specific comportments to being, or to different orientations towards everything that is. They

3. Paul Tillich, *Systematic Theology*, vol. 1, Part II (London, 1951).

each *encompass* everything, and yet do not articulate everything. The particular comportment determines what may be articulated, even though each accounts for everything. By saying each accounts for everything I mean simply that each gives a place to everything. That is different to giving explanation to everything. Cosmologies, in this sense, arise from the immediate sense of the All, while explanation, taking All as given, seeks to discern the specific empirical properties of things. For example, the cosmic myths of the Kalahari Bushmen grant a dwelling place to all things, but in no sense are they the result of empirical enquiry. They are narratives of *living with and amid* the mystery of things.

The kind of knowledge such philosophical reflection gives is therefore quite distinct from the kind of knowledge empirical investigation gives. Philosophical knowledge arises from the *givenness* of things. Such reflection contemplates that which is disclosed by all that is from the disclosing power of being itself. Until our times it was understood that the intellect was the faculty which received that which was disclosed of things themselves, as distinct from the reason, because the intellect is potentially all knowledge.

The question now arises: In what way is religious or theological knowledge distinct from metaphysical knowledge? It would almost seem that such metaphysical knowledge was complete in itself, or even that it was religious. It is clear, however, from the great religious scriptures that religious knowledge transcends all metaphysical knowledge.

In the religious writings of the mystics we discern a threshold beyond which we must go to arrive at the spiritual knowledge of things. This is expressed in innumerable ways, and we need to bear in mind that they are always a manner of speaking of that threshold, and we should not regard them as literal or factual in the ordinary sense. Since we are here concerned with the relations between the different kinds of knowledge, I shall draw upon those expressions which bring out this aspect. In Bonaventure's *Journey of the Mind into God* we are given a threefold series of steps which approximate our division of knowledge into three kinds. He writes:

For we are so created that the material universe itself is a ladder by which we may ascend to God. And among things, some are vestiges, others, images some corporeal, others, spiritual; some temporal, others, everlasting; some things are outside us, and some within. In order to arrive at the consideration of the First Principle, which is wholly spiritual and eternal and above us, we must pass through vestiges which are corporeal and temporal and outside us. Thus we are guided in the way of God. Next we must enter into our mind, which is the image of God—an image which is everlasting, spiritual, and within us. And this is to enter the truth of God. Finally, looking at the First Principle, we must go beyond to what is eternal, absolutely spiritual, and above us.[4]

His threefold division is into the things 'outside' us which the senses perceive, to the things 'within' us, which is an image of God, and finally to that which is 'above' us, which is absolutely spiritual. Bonaventure derives this threefold division from the Divine Trinity, of which the threefold division is itself a reflection. It is characteristic of Bonaventure that his *source* is already theological, and that the Divine Trinity is a key to all things. So although he is tracing the journey of the mind from the knowledge of the visible world to the intelligible world of mind, and from mind to God, he is already regarding the created order as reflecting the divine order. He understands that the Divine Trinity is manifest everywhere, and is disclosed as a 'ladder' of 'vestiges' and 'images' through which the mind passes to the spiritual. This 'passing through' is not an act of *disposing* of the temporal, corporal or visible, but rather of seeing what they *communicate* of the divine. Thus the journey to the spiritual is a procedure tracing the divine in all things, first in the sensible realm, then in the intelligible and finally in the divine itself without mediation. For Bonaventure, as typical in one way or another of all the Christian mystics, God is at once wholly immanent and wholly transcendent. For him the key is

4. Bonaventure, *Journey of the Mind Into God* (*Itinerarium Mentis in Deum*) (Franciscan Institute New York, 1956) 1, 2.

the Divine Trinity which is manifest everywhere as the *manifesting power* of things. Thus there is a 'mystical way' of seeing even the most material things. He makes this point boldly in what he says next, yet shows how such knowledge comes from Scripture:

> This triple way of seeing, then, is the three days' journey in the wilderness, it is the threefold enlightenment of a single day: the first is like evening; the second, morning; and the third, noon day. It reflects the threefold existence of things: in matter, in the understanding, and in the eternal art, according to which it was said: *Let it be made, He made it,* and *it was made.* Finally, it reflects the threefold substance in Christ, Who is our ladder: the corporeal, the spiritual, and the divine substance.[5]

Again we see the way in which Bonaventure discerns the Divine Trinity permeating the Scriptures in the symbolism of the three days' journey in the wilderness and in the threefold substance of Christ, who is the ladder itself. In these two brief quotations from Bonaventure we have a synthesis of Christian theology, of mystical interpretation of Scripture and an absorption of Platonism through the vestiges and images. This is important to note because the mystics are quite often regarded as in some way 'outside' religion, as though the mystical knowledge of things discarded all tradition or culture, when in truth the mystics completely absorb it and wholly synthesize it, though each in some unique way.

That which is religious can be said only religiously. By this we mean that there is no kind of language or mode of understanding which can properly speak of or understand the religious except the religious understanding itself. Any kind of objective, psychological or phenomenological description of the religious leaves aside the essentially religious, because the religious belongs only to itself. This means the religious language, which is essentially symbolic, is the means by

5. *Itinerarium*, 1, 2.

which the religious is disclosed. It is sometimes said that Ultimate Truth cannot be expressed, but from within the religious it is only Ultimate Truth that is fully expressed, while every other kind of truth remains half hidden even when expressed. To put it another way, it is not a matter of whether Ultimate Truth can be expressed or not, but a matter of whether it can be known or not. From the level of mystical knowledge, everything is the expression of Ultimate Truth because that alone is the ground of expressibility itself. Truth is infinitely communicable, and everything else is communicable only in a secondary way compared to this primordial communicability. This relates to our second principle: All things are in communion with all other things. This communion of all things is the completion of communicability. When it is claimed that Ultimate Truth cannot be expressed what is really in question here is whether it can be expressed separately from itself, in a form other than itself. Nevertheless, from the mystical level *everything* is the full expression of Ultimate Truth, because there is nothing else expressed.

This means that any effort to grasp Ultimate Truth by any mode of knowledge other than through its own communicability is really an effort to grasp it other than as itself. That is to say, the knowing agent is God Himself in the soul, not the soul knowing God. It is God's own knowledge of Himself that is communicated to the soul. And since God's knowledge of Himself *is* Himself it cannot be communicated as other than Himself. Although this may sound extravagant, really it is not.[6] Each realm of knowledge has its own characteristic manner of being known. The empirical realm is known through scientific method and demonstration, and such knowledge is communicated in that way among those who share that knowledge. Likewise with metaphysical knowledge: it cannot be translated into empirical knowledge, as we have seen already. And so it is with religious or mystical knowledge: it is known only directly or not at all. For Bonaventure *everything is expressing God*, the wholly spiritual, and so for man it is a

6. This absolute communicability of God to the soul is especially elaborated by Meister Eckhart.

matter of coming to see what is already fully disclosed. But the final step involves a transformation of the soul by God.

However, there is an important characteristic to be observed about these three orders of knowledge which we have not yet touched upon. The kind of knowledge which is gained through scientific method comes only by the application of that method and, strictly speaking, is accessible to those only who come to it by that same method. To judge of a scientific truth is possible only through the scientific method. It is therefore communicable only to insiders, to those with the specialist knowledge and method. Metaphysical knowledge, on the other hand, is open to all because, as we noted earlier, the human being is the being who reflects on being. All that is required is that the mind addresses itself to the meaning of being. All the philosophical literature is likewise open to everyone, and so any individual can share in the accumulated reflection of man on the question of being. So, by comparison with the empirical knowledge of things, metaphysical knowledge may be immediately known and is the more communicable. The only requirement is the clear capacity to reflect without confusion.

If we follow through this direction of thought, we see that religious or mystical knowledge is yet more open to being known, because it is the knowledge which is wholly self-communicating or self-disclosing. Yet it is neither inferential knowledge, as in the sciences, nor reflective knowledge, as in metaphysics, but Ultimate Truth knowing itself, or participation in the divine knowledge, the act of God knowing Himself in the soul, as Meister Eckhart says. It is an order of knowledge in which there is no object known or subject knowing, mystically expressed as 'Divine darkness'. It may be said to be arrived at through a negation of all other things, including the distinctness of the knower, or through a total inclusiveness of all things in which unity and differentiation are distinct and yet one. Bonaventure, in the final step of the ascent of the mind, conceives it as perfect knowledge of the unity of the Divine Trinity:

Once more retracing our steps, let us say that because the most pure and absolute being which is unqualifiedly being is the first and the last, it is therefore the origin and the consummating end of all things. As eternal and most present, it encompasses and enters all duration, existing, as it were, at one and the same time as their centre and their circumference. Likewise, because it is the most simple and the greatest, it is wholly within all things and wholly outside them; hence it is 'an intelligible sphere, whose centre is everywhere and whose circumference is nowhere'. As most actual and changeless, it is that which, 'remaining unmoved itself, gives movement to all things'. Further, because it is most perfect and immense, it is within all things without being contained by them, outside all things without being excluded, above all things without being aloof, below all things without being dependent. Finally, since it is supremely one and yet omnifarious, it is *all in all,* even though all things are many and it is itself but one. And this is so because through its supremely simple unity, its most serene truth, and its most sincere goodness, it contains in itself all power, all exemplarity, and all communicability. Hence *from him and through him and unto him are all things . . . .*[7]

By this ascent of the mind through the perception of outward things, then through the inward perception of the mind, and finally to the contemplation of the Divine in Itself above the mind, Bonaventure represents the journey as *inclusive of all things.* This is characteristic of Franciscan mysticism, in which the truth, the actuality and the good-ness of all things are known only in knowing things in God. For Bonaventure the *via positiva* and the *via negativa* completely con-verge. This is because the ascent of the soul begins in affirming the reflected presence (*via positiva*) of the Trinity and moves towards the actual presence of the Trinity. Leaving behind the reflected presence (*via negativa*) it comes to a fuller presence within itself (*via positiva*), and then, going above itself (*via negativa*) it arrives at God fully communicating Himself (*via positiva*). The reason Bonaventure departs from the usual sequence of ascent as formulated by Dionysius the

7. *Itinerarium* 5, 8.

Areopagite, in which the *via positiva* is followed by the *via negativa*, is because his mysticism of ascent is an ascent towards the *infinite communicability* of God. To put that another way, for Bonaventure the soul does not ascend by its own power but entirely by the communicable power of the Divine Trinity. In this way it transcends metaphysics and becomes religious.

There is an aspect of the journey which is of particular interest in the context of the kinds of knowledge we have been discussing. This is the mind's recollection of itself as made in the image of God at the fourth step:

> Since we contemplate the First Principle not only through us on our way, but also in us, and since this kind of consideration is more excellent than the former, therefore it holds the fourth step in contemplation. It seems strange indeed that after what has been shown of God's closeness to our souls there are so few concerned about perceiving the First Principle within themselves. Distracted by many cares, the human mind does not enter into itself through the memory; beclouded by sense images, it does not come back to itself through the intelligence; and drawn away by the concupiscences, it does not return to itself through the desire for interior sweetness and spiritual joy. Therefore, completely immersed in things of sense, the soul cannot re-enter into itself as the image of God.[8]

In Medieval thought the memory[9] was often considered to be the highest power of the mind, higher even than the intellect. It is so understood in *The Cloud of Unknowing*. Clearly, this is to be understood as

8. *Itinerarium* 4, 1.

9. The precedence given to memory over intellect by some Christian mystics is derived from the Platonic strand. For Plato all real knowledge is recollection. The precedence given to the intellect, on the other hand, is derived from Aristotle. For Aristotle it is the intellect that is oriented towards the truth of things. This is most fully taken up by Aquinas, for whom intellect participates in the unity of things. However, it must be borne in mind that Bonaventure represents Franciscan theology which is founded on an understanding of the immediate divine presence of the Trinity and the full communicability of God. Aquinas represents Dominican theology which

memory in the Platonic sense and not in the everyday modern sense of recollection of facts or experience. It is at once the power to which all the other powers (the will, the reason and the five senses) are directed, but also the power in which the mind recollects itself. However, once distracted by sense images and desires, it may return to itself only through grace. This raises an important question about the higher modes of knowledge.

From a simple rational point of view, it seems strange that the mind cannot know itself of itself, especially in our times when, as we discussed earlier, knowledge is conceived of as at the command of the human will. But if we recall the third of the propositions discussed in our previous lectures this can begin to make sense: all things disclose their nature as an act of their being. This metaphysical principle comes from the yet higher theological principle: that all things disclose themselves as an act of their being because they arise into being as an act of God's self-communicability. Or, as Aquinas puts it, all things come into being through being known into being in the mind of God. In God, self-communion is the same as knowing and being. But also, God's act of self-knowing is the same as knowing all things into being. The act of creation is essentially an act of divine self-disclosure, and the divine act of self-disclosure arises from God's self-communion. It follows from this that for the human mind to recollect itself it must in some sense participate in God's act of knowing it into being. But also, in Bonaventure's terms, if the mind is to come to knowledge of God it must be conformed to a likeness of God, since knowledge of God is a participation in the divine knowledge. Thus the mind must know itself in the image of God. This participation is by grace,

----

is founded on the contemplative life of learning. The Franciscans tended to see learning as an obstacle to the spiritual life, even to the point of seeing literacy as a vice. Bonaventure was given the task of reconciling the conflict between learning and spirituality in the Franciscan Order, and *The Journey of the Mind Into God* was written by him in response to this conflict.

The precedence of memory is also to be found in Augustine's Trinitarian psychology in which the memory is associated with the Father, understanding with the Son, and will with the Holy Spirit.

because the movement of knowing comes from God, not from the mind. The mind does not need to move to God because God is already present or, as St Paul puts it, God is already all in all.

In describing this order of knowledge Bonaventure has called upon the symbolic language of Scripture and the classical language of metaphysics. In doing this he is following the theological discourse of the Middle Ages. It is understood that, when used theologically, the language of metaphysics becomes metaphorical. This is not because there is no adequate language for theological understanding, or that language is limited, but because language itself is ultimately the Word of God speaking God, and is therefore no longer language as representation or description. From the mystical perspective all things are the disclosure of God and are present only by virtue of the divine presence which is the presencing act in itself. The popular notion that language is finite and limited, and therefore must fall short of speaking of God, is itself a non-religious or non-theological notion of language. Theologically, language does not speak *of* God but *speaks God Himself*. Really, nothing else is ever being uttered but God. In this regard language is no different from any other manifestation. From the religious perspective all things disclose God, and that disclosure is their essential act of being. Everything is mystical union. That is what the mystic sees. It is this that makes all things actual, both in themselves, to themselves, and to all other things.

Although it may be controversial to say so, truly religious understanding is this mystical order of knowledge. Religion conceived as 'belief systems', as 'doctrines' or 'moral precepts' and so on, are distorted views of religion, secular notions of religion, religion conceived outside its own terms. This way of looking at religion has largely come about by the separation of religion from metaphysics (which is not to say they are the same), or rather the general abandonment of metaphysics in modern thought through reducing it to mere system. So we are left with the empirical sciences on the one hand and 'religious belief' on the other, and subsequently both are spoken of in terms of the 'factual'. Without the metaphysical realm of knowledge between, both religion and science become blind and without ground or direction. The sciences become ends in themselves without regard for their proper part within the natural order of things, and religion becomes merely private conviction in irresolvable conflict with the prevailing materialist world-view. The only way out of this situation, it seems to me, is to begin to attend again to that which shows itself in the very presence of things and to begin to think from that natural harmony of reality which we intuitively know but do not know how to articulate. This is the calling of philosophy, which commences from the perception of the intelligence manifest in reality itself.

We have tried to distinguish three orders of knowledge, the Empirical, the Metaphysical and the Religious. The first comes through inference and is verified by inference. The second comes by insight and is not verifiable except in terms of itself. The third comes through the pure communicability of things as an act of revelation. This last is already given and yet is known only through coming to the divine ground from whence all things arise into being. The three orders of knowledge, seen in this way, are three orders of receptivity to that which is disclosed. There is not a complete discontinuity between the orders of knowledge, yet they are quite distinct and confusion arises if they are mixed together, or if one tries to speak on behalf of another. One wonders, however, what might be disclosed if the sciences were undertaken in the awareness of metaphysics, and if metaphysics were undertaken in the awareness of divine knowledge. This is a question we shall try to address in the final lecture.

4

Loss and Recovery of Metaphysics

ॐ

I N the three preceding lectures I have tried to bring to light the differences between the three orders of knowledge, and how confusion arises if these are mixed together. I have tried to make it clear that empirical knowledge can never answer metaphysical questions, and even less theological or religious questions. In the last lecture we asked if these three kinds of knowledge could be undertaken in the light or awareness of one another. It seems to me that this is a most important question in our time. One reason for this is that with the tendency towards ever greater specialization, each field of knowledge becomes more and more oblivious of the others, and with that there comes an assumption that all kinds of knowledge are on the same flat plane. For example, undergraduates are often taught in the sciences and social sciences that 'religion' is simply the historical predecessor of scientific knowledge, as if religion were just a primitive form of scientific knowledge.

This oblivion of the meaning of religion is startling. But even more disconcerting in such a view is the oblivion of the meaning of knowledge itself. The confidence that is evident in the exclusive pursuit of empirical knowledge is founded upon unspoken presuppositions about the nature of reality and the nature of the human relation to reality. These unspoken presuppositions about the nature of knowledge and reality are themselves metaphysical in essence, but are not known to be so and are not examined in their own right. Metaphysics is assumed not to exist. Thus, generally speaking, the nature of the prevailing modern world-view is not really seen at all. It is not scientific method itself that is the problem, but the lack of understanding of what kind of engagement with reality it involves. A consequence of this lack of understanding is a great deal of bad science, of explanations of things in the name of science which are themselves scientifically unsound. The lack of reflection on the nature of knowledge undermines the sciences themselves.

The problem is really a philosophical one, in so far as philosophy is the exploration of the meaning of being and the meaning of knowing. Philosophy stands mediately between scientific knowledge and mystical knowledge. It reflects on what it means to be and to know, and it is this peculiar power of reflection that distinguishes the human species from the other species in nature. Without this reflection all human endeavours are blind and without real ground, and the result of this is growing alienation from reality and fragmentation of civilization. The capacity to *participate* in the world is decreased. In such a situation it becomes a preoccupation of governments and of law-making to try and curb the ill-effects of this alienation. And for most people 'meaning' is sought in fleeting distractions—in consumerism, in drugs, in superficial entertainment, in fanaticism. The alienation without is complemented by an alienation within. The 'meaningless world' is matched by the vacant self, the self with no ground, no vocation and no nature or essence.

In the second lecture we touched upon the loss of the idea or understanding of natural law. Plato, we recall, sought to understand how human law was a natural extension of the laws of nature, and Aquinas sought to understand the relation between human law and divine law. It was once understood that there was a continuation and correspondence between nature and human society, and that an understanding of this correspondence was a key to situating humanity within the cosmos. Here is a point of convergence between modern scientific knowledge of the highly complex order of nature and the natural knowledge of every individual that intuits that everything has its place in the total design of things. But this sense of order is not sufficiently reflected upon. Rather than reflect on what it may be disclosing to us, all effort is expended on trying to manipulate nature according to our unquestioned desires. The quest for control over nature conceals the subtle knowledge of nature from us.

Given this situation, I would like to take just one metaphysical insight found in Plato and Aristotle and which endured in one form or another throughout the Middle Ages. It is the principle that all beings seek the good of full actualization, and that the good of each being contributes to and harmonizes with the total good of all things. In this simple principle we have a ground for the source of all natural desires, for all natural growth or development, for the quest for knowledge and even for ultimate mystical union. The implications of such a principle are so enormous that we can hardly imagine the infinite flowering that could spring from it, and yet it is a principle which anyone can grasp, a principle which everyone knows in their bones, so to speak. Applied to human society, here is one simple implication: that every human talent or vocation has its natural place within the total order of society. That is to say, nature has ordained all things in such a way that each human being has a unique part to play in the natural flowering of society. Each talent or vocation is related to the whole, and fulfils the calling of the individual and the general good simultaneously. The good of the whole and the good of the individual reinforce and sustain one another. Such mutual good is the basis of real social participation.

This may sound idealistic, but actually it is simply natural within the larger fabric of nature if we grant intelligence back to it as the philosophers once did. In metaphysical terms it is what nature seeks. In physical terms it is the nature of society. In political terms it is possible, however, only if it is understood. This is important. As we said a moment ago, the human being is the being who reflects, and if the call to reflect is unheeded then the natural flowering of society and the individual is not possible. The law of the good must be understood—which means it must be discerned, not merely hoped for or propagated as an ideology.

Given this natural law, we may see something else very important: that the fragmentation and alienation of the present world is itself the natural and lawful consequence of ignoring natural law. The intellectual fragmentation in the universities, the confusion in the arts, the drift of religion towards legalism or fanaticism, the destruction of the environment, poverty, inequality, global warming and so on, are all signs of departing from this simple natural law. The natural law is showing itself plainly in all these ills. If there were no natural order, then these ills would not appear. Nature would be indifferent and there would be no consequences. None of our present ills are caused by nature, but by man's disregard of nature.

I believe this is obvious to most people, even though it may not be understood in a clear or precise way. This brings us to another important philosophical point about thought itself in our time. There is a disparity in our age between how we conceive reality and how it discloses itself to us. We recall here Aquinas's epistemological principle: all things are oriented toward being known. That is to say, everything discloses its nature, its essence, in the manner of its being. The coming into being of things *is* a showing of essence. It is of the nature of being to reveal itself. Correspondingly, it is of the nature of mind to receive the revealing of being. The human intelligence receives the intelligence of the whole of reality. In this sense man is the being through whom nature reflects upon itself. This is a principle that was understood in Western philosophy from classical Greek times until the Enlightenment. Since then the disparity between the general conception of reality and how it discloses itself has increasingly marked. This is reflected in the objectifying language we see adopted everywhere from the empirical sciences. This language strips everything of its immediate meaning and places things at the disposal of human command. I am not criticizing the sciences here, but simply noting that the notion of 'objective truth' has been uncritically absorbed into practically all realms of thought, so that the objective concept displaces that which shows itself of things. We see it everywhere, not only in academic discourse, but in the modern language of business, in economics, in social analysis, in ecology, in education theory, in art theory, and in the endless coinage of abbreviations. This objectifying language projects the illusion of command over things while in truth it clearly reflects disengagement and alienation, including alienation from language itself. The alienation is widely felt, and yet the attention given to alienation itself only compounds the alienation through the language applied to it—the 'underclass', the 'economically deprived', the 'socially excluded', 'the minority', the 'victim of oppression' and so on. This kind of language appears to grasp things, yet it is powerless to accomplish anything because there is no natural whole to which all is related. And so the natural language of belonging to the human family—the simple language of friendship, of comradeship, of loyalty, of compassion, of love, of kinship, of enthusiasm, of dedication—is displaced by the objectifying language of human rights, of litigation, of demand and so on.

Nevertheless, this objectifying language is itself revealing the disparity between conceiving and what discloses itself. Language never lies. Our manner of relating to the world is reflected precisely in the language that prevails. The objectifying manner of speaking is already a stance towards everything that is, and this is concealed by the belief that objective language is faithful to the truth of things behind their appearances. It is believed, without any reflection, that nothing discloses itself directly, that there is no simple connection between perception and the actual presence of things.

This situation has not passed unnoticed by modern philosophers. The school of phenomenology, initiated by Husserl, has tried to return to how things show themselves. But this school of thought has subsequently turned into a kind of reductionism and become preoccupied with trying to elaborate itself rather than bring the showing of things to light, and in much scholarship that speaks in its name it has become objectifying without noticing it. As seems to happen with many modern insights, they become systems disengaged from their original ground.

The problem of objectification is a peculiar problem of our times. This is not to say that all was well in previous ages. Nevertheless, Western philosophy has always been concerned with the relation of reality and language. It was always understood that there is a true correspondence between the truth of things and language, and that language can faithfully speak the truth of things. But this correspondence was never supposed to be a simple correlation between sign and signified, as if the word were simply a label for things.

One cannot approach language through objectifying thought, through analysis of semiotics and so on. As we have already seen, human speaking embodies a comportment to reality. If I may put it so, every word we speak is our *reply* to existence. Like Adam in Genesis, we stand before all things and are called upon to name them, and howsoever we name things, that is our witness to being, our witness to truth. We may put this more strongly: to speak is to dedicate. Every word we utter is ultimately an offering to God. It seems to me that we can get at human language only by going all the way back to what moves us to speak, because all speaking is an act of affirmation of what we hold to be true or of value. Thus trying to understand language in terms of signs separated from a speaker is already to miss language completely. Likewise, to take language as merely what it means to me personally is to miss language completely. To fully hear the spoken word is to hear a dedication. It may be to hear the word of love or it may be to hear the word of a fanatic, yet it is a dedication. And so likewise with the authoritative word of science, of string theory or the latest notion of genetic determination. These are all essentially words of dedication. All depends, then, on what the act of dedication is dedicated to, and how we hear the dedication. If language in our time is dedicated to the objectifying enterprise, then we need to reflect on how this enterprise misses the truth of things, or how it substitutes itself as the truth of things, or how the notion of 'objective truth' has occurred and taken hold of our culture.

I do not think we can understand how this has happened if we do not ask the fundamental philosophical question: what calls to be known? Nothing calls to be objectified, yet the truth of things calls to be known. This call does not come from our desire to know, but from the truth or presence of things which awakens the desire to know. Therefore to seek to know is a response to the truth of things, which shows itself in the natural human inclination to give regard to things. To give no regard is to be less than human. The word regard means 'to keep, heed, or mark' and the suffix 're-' means 'again'. To keep means to 'have the care of', to 'guard', to 'maintain', 'hold' or 'preserve'.[1] Therefore to regard the truth of things means to tend and protect and care for them for the sake of the truth itself. This is the opposite to setting reality at human disposal or command, which is essentially the aim of the objectifying enterprise.

This is a revealing reversal. In seeking objective command over things man alienates himself from reality. In trying to secure himself through subduing the world, he denies that which reality bestows upon him of itself out of its abundance. And yet even this is still a manner of regarding the truth of things.

The genuine question of the philosopher asks 'What calls to be known?' This question places us in a kind of not knowing, or in an intermediate place between knowing and not knowing. It brings into question how we attend to reality. It asks of an order of knowledge that is itself a response to things. And it asks about the relation of mind and thought to reality. These are questions that have followed us through these lectures.

Here I would like to suggest a dimension to human reflection which is easily passed over. In the last lecture we saw how the myth of the Tower of Babel resulted in the confusion of tongues, and we interpreted this in a twofold way. First, the confusion of tongues signified everyone speaking their own language which others could not understand and second, that for each individual this signified a split between the heart and the power of speech. The myth suggests that human understanding is a collective act. This does not mean that individuals do not understand in themselves, but it does mean that the highest knowledge requires the human community, that there is an order of knowledge that is possible only through collective reflection.

In a way this is obvious. The knowledge and wisdom transmitted through tradition is what forms the foundation of human community in each generation. The human society is by nature possible only through an assent to commonly held truths and values. This 'knowing in common' is the ground upon which human enquiry can take place. Plato says that real knowledge can arise only through

1. W. W. Skeat, *Etymological Dictionary of the English Language* (Oxford, 1989).

dialogue. We all know from experience how insights arise through discussion. This obvious fact contains within itself a remarkable principle, and one wonders why it is not generally recognized: there is a correlation between the depth of communal understanding and the flowering of civilization. In an age when the autonomy of the individual is held in such high esteem one wonders why it is not recognized that, without membership of the community of mankind, there is no possibility of the autonomy of the individual. Individual liberty and community are two faces of one thing. The autonomy of the individual resides in the capacity to participate in the greater human community, and beyond that to participate in the greater unfoldment of the totality of reality. Such participation occurs, however, only at the level of intellectual reflection. Community is essentially community of mind.

Earlier we observed that, according to natural law, every human talent or vocation had its place in the design of nature, and that this offered a key to understanding the nature of society, or at least to its potential actualization. But this is a possibility only if understood. There is a call, in the very nature of things, for humanity to understand the nature of the unity of the human race. If one thinks about it, this unity is the real basis of the formulation of human laws. Good laws facilitate unity, while bad laws fragment.

If community is essentially community of mind, then language lies at the heart of community. The principle institutions of any society are manifestations of the word and exist through the word. Government, religion, education, jurisprudence and so on all exist through language, and act through the word. Through these institutions the depth of human understanding manifests itself. This is why it is so vital that there is no corruption in these institutions. Here language manifests itself most clearly as dedication, and dedication here corresponds with virtue, with integrity, honesty and truthfulness.

It seems extraordinary to me that the social and political sciences have not yet observed that the principle institutions of society are essentially the spoken word. So much attention has been given to systems, bureaucracy and class differences that the primacy of language

has been overlooked. The institutions are not systems but intelligences, and that is why they are so powerful. But more than this,
they are the intelligences within society which act in relation to the
whole of society, and which represent the action of society in relation
to the whole of reality. The key here is unity, or the manner in which
unity is understood. In law it is the unity of justice, in education the
unity of knowledge, and in religion the unity of truth or goodness.
Each of these unities are open to inexhaustible reflection, and therefore have unlimited potential.[2]

Although these are very subtle matters, nevertheless every human
being knows them at heart. All recognize that real knowledge must be
united because reality itself is a unity, and all recognize that law must
be grounded in justice because justice opens the way to the boundless
possibilities of human action and participation, and all recognize that
any human work worthy of being undertaken must be oriented
towards ultimate truth and goodness. These are the real ground of
human aspiration and idealism, and they encompass everything from
the humblest duty to the highest mystical union. In the recognition of
these naturally intuited principles lies the recognition of that which
calls to be known.

In the previous lecture we posed the question 'what might be disclosed if the sciences were undertaken in the awareness of metaphysics, and if metaphysics were undertaken in the awareness of divine
knowledge?' In the light of these observations it seems clear that so
long as the different modes of knowledge are undertaken in isolation
from one another they cannot properly fulfil their real ends. But are
they in fact isolated?

In so far as the scientific undertaking is the application of method
or technique it is no different from the application of any other
method or technique. But in so far as it claims to gain knowledge of
things, it immediately enters the realm of metaphysics as a mode of

2. It is important to understand we are speaking here in principle about the nature
of society, in terms of social ontology. The fact that we may live in a time when the
nature of human society is not understood or ignored does not alter the principle.

knowledge, and as a mode of knowledge it may be questioned as a type of communion with reality. Once questioned in this way it cannot justify itself as merely the application of method or technique, as though method had no wider implications beyond itself. Technique is not in itself an act of knowledge or knowing, and the knowledge that arises from technique exists on another plane, and this plane comes within the provenance of philosophical reflection.

It is precisely here that Western philosophy has been confused, although that is perhaps now beginning to change. For a long time philosophy, seeing the effectiveness of the sciences and technology, attempted to model itself on scientific technique, and so practically all thinking gravitated to enquiry into the empirical and measurable realm. The rise of modern science was accompanied by the decline of philosophy. Essentially, what has occurred is that the meaning and essence of the sciences was not reflected upon, and that the strange and disconcerting problems we now face with the rule of technology in practically every field of human activity is due to a failure of philosophical reflection.

Consequently the scientific discoveries of the mechanics of things have been taken to be the *meaning* of things. It is this extrapolation of scientific facts into the realm of meaning that leads to the common belief that scientific knowledge discloses the essence of things. It is this belief, for example, that underlies the current confusion about the ethics of genetic manipulation. Intuitively most people know this is wrong, but there is no philosophical language or discourse in which this knowledge can be properly articulated. The truth of the known cannot be said. This inarticulacy itself reveals the profound importance of language as belonging to the essence of society. It is a salutary example of the disparity between the modern conception of reality and the nature of reality itself discussed in our previous lecture concerning the pre-intuition of totality and bringing this pre-intuition to reflective understanding and articulation.

A similar event has occurred within the religious dimension. Theology has largely retreated into the realm of private subjectivity or doctrinalism. As subjectivity it is little more than feeling or sensibility, and therefore easily dismissed as wishful thinking by opponents: as doctrinalism it has become merely an instrument for claiming the authority of supernatural revelation. As either of these it cannot adequately reflect on philosophy or scientific knowledge, and so contributes to the fragmentation of understanding.

And yet everyone has a pre-intuitive sense that there is an infinite mystery which underlies everything and to which all things ultimately belong. It is this openness to the infinite mystery which makes immediate reality discernible and which tells us that everything that exists is naturally sacred. Even philosophy, ultimately, grants that there is a sanctity about the being and truth of things, and that the quest for knowledge and understanding springs from a reverence for truth which surpasses knowledge itself. This love of truth, which belongs to man by nature, is ultimately unconditional because it loves that which is unconditional. It is at this point that we arrive at the fourth proposition in our first lecture: that man is called to bear witness to the truth of things. This principle runs through each of the three orders of knowledge, given that they are undertaken in conformity with human nature.

This intuitive knowledge of the infinite mystery which underlies everything really comes first in the orders of knowledge. That is to say, the religious openness to the infinite underlying everything is the prerequisite to philosophical contemplation if philosophy is to have its full scope; and the philosophical contemplation is the prerequisite to scientific investigation if the sciences are to remain open to what nature discloses of itself. Given this natural order—which was the order understood in classical Greek philosophy and in the establishment of the European universities—the empirical sciences are no longer detached from the contemplation of the unity of reality as a whole, and religion is no longer confined to private subjectivity but holds to its original sense of unconditional dedication to the unconditional ground and meaning of all things as they exist in the mind of the Creator.

This does not mean that religion critiques philosophy, or that philosophy critiques science.[3] It means, rather, that the quest for knowledge is oriented towards the truth of things in accordance with the good of things in themselves. Instead of being reduced to the merely useful—the modern justification for knowledge—the pursuit of knowledge becomes an honouring and sanctification of reality.

The fact that religion, philosophy and science are not presently understood in this way does not change their intrinsic nature. We are speaking here in terms of their real essence. The problems we have addressed in each one of them are not problems inherent in them as such, but rather they are problems that have arisen through misconceiving them. Put simply, to a large degree they are presently thought to be different from what they actually are, and it is this which underlies the wrong relations between them. In particular, it is through misconceptions about the nature of technology that leads to pollution and harm to the environment. Technology does not do this of itself, any more than religion produces fanatics of itself. It is the manner in which modern man conceives his relation to the cosmos as a whole that leads to harming the environment, and thus to the abuse of knowledge. Locating the problem in technology is itself part of the prevailing technological view of things. Of itself technology is neither a problem nor a solution to a problem. That is like blaming a knife for committing a murder.

The real problem lies in the circumscribed view of reality that prevails in our age. We can trace this back to various shifts in

3. By this I mean that philosophy is already self-critical in its dialectical nature. Therefore it can be challenged effectively only through philosophical meditation. That is precisely what Plato does in the Dialogues. To critique philosophy necessitates *doing* philosophy. The same principle holds with scientific method in so far as it is method. Faulty scientific method is exposed by science itself. However, religion can elect to ignore philosophy, but theology cannot do this in so far as it is concerned with the nature of being and knowing. Likewise, both theology and philosophy can examine the manner in which the practice of science is concerned with truth or goodness because scientific method does not, of itself, determine the kind of knowledge that ought to be sought or the morality of its practice. In short, the *application* of scientific method, or technology, in any specific act is informed by values outside its method, and values belong to the realms of philosophical reflection and theological interpretation.

theological and philosophical thinking that began in the late Middle Ages, such as the rise of nominalism and the shift from an ontological understanding of God to that of divine will which we touched on earlier, both of which eventually divorced nature from Grace.

Nevertheless, the narrow, fixed view of reality is beginning to lose its hold. This is certainly the case in the best of modern philosophy[4] and in some theology.[5] The complacent certitude of most nineteenth-century scholarship now appears to us as absurdly arrogant. We are becoming more aware that reality cannot so easily be taken hold of and that it is much more subtle than was supposed by the logical positivists. But perhaps the most significant change underway is in the scholarly understanding of ancient Greek and Medieval thought which has long been interpreted through the presuppositions of Enlightenment Rationalism.[6] Philosophy is beginning to resituate itself within the whole of the Western tradition once again, leaving behind the philosophical provincialism of the last several hundred years. This is a movement in the contrary direction to the ever increasing specialization that has dominated learning for so long.

But aside from these hopeful signs within academic scholarship there is in Western society generally a growing sense that the prevailing materialistic values lack real depth or meaning, and that the cosmos cannot be a mere accident hurtling its way to a final extinction. That narrow mechanistic view runs contrary to the felt mystery of things. But more blatantly than this the ecological crisis calls for a united human response to nature as a whole. One might say that the threat of human extinction is nature's reply to treating it as a mere

4. For example Logical Positivism, which grounded itself in the epistemology of empirical rationalism, has been shown to have hidden ontological presuppositions which challenge its claim to be purely epistemological. The assumption that philosophy could be conducted as a type of pure logical reasoning wholly independent of any ontology has broken down within philosophy itself.

5. For example the Radical Orthodoxy school of theology is challenging the secular view of politics. See John Milbank, *Theology & Social Theory: Beyond Secular Reason* (Blackwell, 1993).

6. See for example David Roochnik, *Of Art and Wisdom: Plato's Understanding of Techne* (Pennsylvania, 1996).

resource for human manipulation and consumption. Human alienation from the greater whole is not granted by the natural order. Seen
in this light the necessity to attend to the whole is a call from providence to dwell more fully within nature. This call is not answered by
merely saving energy or becoming more efficient, but by a reorienta-
tion of human dedication towards reality as such at every level. It is
this that can bring about the proper relations between the orders of
knowledge. All human work could become meaningful if undertaken
in this spirit, and that would be the *natural* state of society, a state
wholly in harmony with the divine cosmic order.

Bibliography

⧲⧲

Aquinas, Thomas, *Commentary on Aristotle's Metaphysics*, translated by John P. Rowan (Dumb Ox Books, Notre Dame, Indiana, 1995)
—*Summa Theologica* (Eyre & Spotiswoode, London, 1970)
Blasi, Fulvio Di, *God and Natural Law: A Rereading of Thomas Aquinas* (Indiana, 2006)
Bonaventure, *Journey of the Mind Into God (Itinerarium Mentis in Deum)* (Franciscan Institute New York, 1956)
Dupré, Louis, *Passage to Modernity* (Yale, 1993)
Eriugena, *Periphyseon*, translated by John O'Meara (Bellarmin, Montreal, 1987)
Heidegger, Martin, *The Question Concerning Technology and Other Essays* (Harper, 1977)
MacIntyre, Alasdair, *After Virtue* (Duckworth, 1985)
Milbank, John, *Theology & Social Theory: Beyond Secular Reason* (Blackwell, 1993)
Morris, Simon Conway, *Life's Solution: Inevitable Humans in a Lonely Universe* (Cambridge, 2003)
Pagels, Elaine, *The Johannine Gospel in Gnostic Exegesis* (Nashville & New York, 1973)
Pieper, Josef, *Living the Truth* (Ignatius Press, 1989)
Ricoeur, Paul, *Figuring the Sacred* (Minneapolis, 1995)
Ricoeur, Paul, and Jean-Pierre Changuex, *What makes us Think?* (Princeton, 2000)
Roochnik, David, *Of Art and Wisdom: Plato's Understanding of Techne*, (Pennsylvania, 1996)
Skeat, W. W., *Etymological Dictionary of the English Language*, (Oxford, 1989)
Swedenborg, *Arcana Coelestia*, vol. 11 (London, 1978)
Tillich, Paul, *Systematic Theology*, vol. 1, (London, 1951)

THE TEMENOS ACADEMY

An Academy for Education in the light of the Spirit

The Temenos Academy is an educational charity which aims to offer education in philosophy and the arts in the light of the sacred traditions of East and West. The word 'temenos' means 'a sacred precinct'.

Each year the Academy runs up to a hundred lectures and seminars, and occasional film screenings and readings. These range from major public events to small study groups. Our activities are based in London and are open to all.

The Academy publishes a high-quality journal, the *Temenos Academy Review* and other publications in the Temenos Academy Papers series. Over three hundred lectures are available on tape. By these means those unable to attend meetings in London can have access to our work.

The Temenos Academy
PO Box 203
ASHFORD
Kent TN25 5ZT

Tel. 01233 813663
www.temenosacademy.org